Christ, God's Companionship with Man

Christ, God's Companionship with Man

LUIGI GIUSSANI

Excerpts selected and presented by
Julián Carrón

McGill-Queen's University Press
Montreal & Kingston • London • Chicago

All texts by Luigi Giussani and Julián Carrón are
© Fraternità di Comunione e Liberazione, Milano

English edition © McGill-Queen's University Press 2015

ISBN 978-0-7735-4566-3 (paper)
ISBN 978-0-7735-9730-3 (ePDF)
ISBN 978-0-7735-9731-0 (ePUB)

Legal deposit third quarter 2015
Bibliothèque nationale du Québec
Reprinted 2015

Printed in Canada on acid-free paper that is 100% ancient forest free (100% post-consumer recycled), processed chlorine free

McGill-Queen's University Press acknowledges the support of the Canada Council for the Arts for our publishing program. We also acknowledge the financial support of the Government of Canada through the Canada Book Fund for our publishing activities.

Copyright page continues on page 119

Library and Archives Canada Cataloguing in Publication

Giussani, Luigi
[Cristo compagnia di Dio all'uomo. English]
    Christ, God's companionship with man / Luigi Giussani ; excerpts selected and presented by Julián Carrón.

Translation of: Cristo compagnia di Dio all'uomo.
Includes bibliographical references.
Issued in print and electronic formats.
ISBN 978-0-7735-4566-3 (pbk.). – ISBN 978-0-7735-9730-3 (ePDF). –
ISBN 978-0-7735-9731-0 (ePUB)

    1. Spiritual life – Catholic Church. 2. Jesus Christ. I. Carrón, Julián, editor II. Title. III. Title: Cristo compagnia di Dio all'uomo. English

BX2350.3.G47713 2015   248.4'82   C2015-901392-5
                                                 C2015-901393-3

This book was typeset by True to Type in 12/15 Bembo

Contents

Introduction 3

1 The Religious Sense 17

2 Traces of the Christian Experience 25

3 At the Origin of the Christian Claim 32

4 Why the Church? 39

5 The Risk of Education 51

6 Prayer 58

7 Christ, Who Begs for Man's Heart 69

8 "Woman, Do Not Weep!" 75

9 "Simon, Do You Love Me?" 79

10 Charity: The Gift of the Self, Moved 86

11 Christ, God's Companionship with Man 96

12 How We Become Christians 103

13 You Are the Living Fountain of Hope 110

    Notes 115

    Permissions 119

Christ, God's Companionship with Man

Introduction

"Everything happened to me in a completely ordinary way, and the things that happened, as they happened, inspired wonder in me, because it was God who brought them about, weaving from them a history that was happening – and is still happening – in front of my eyes. What I saw happening was the birth of a people in the name of Christ, who is the protagonist of the story."[1] With these words, spoken on the day of his eightieth birthday, Fr Giussani summarized his entire life – he was seized by Christ from the time he was just a boy, and therefore was able to generate life in others. This is how he was remembered by then Cardinal Joseph Ratzinger when he celebrated Giussani's funeral Mass on 24 February 2005, in the Duomo in Milan: "Fr Giussani was adamant that he didn't want to live for himself; rather, he gave his life, and exactly in this way found life not only for himself but also for many others. He practiced what we heard in the Gospel: he did not want to be served but to serve, he was a faithful servant of the Gospel, he gave out all the wealth of his heart, he gave out all the divine wealth of the Gospel with which he was penetrated and, serving in this way, giving his life, this life of his bore rich fruit – as we see in this moment – he has become really father of many and, having led people not to himself but to Christ, he really won hearts; he has helped to make the world better and to open the world's doors for heaven."[2]

Luigi Giussani was born in Desio, in Brianza, Italy, on 15 October 1922. His father Beniamino, who had socialist sympathies, was an artist and a carpenter; his mother Angelina, a devout Catholic, worked in a textile factory. Fr Giussani always spoke of having assimilated some of his decisive attitudes about life at home. From his father, he learned to demand to know the reasons behind things, a sense of justice and a love for music; from his mother he gained the conviction that faith is a new gaze on all things. He remembers, as a boy, hearing her say, "How beautiful is the world, and how great is God!" as they walked to Mass early one morning while the last stars still shone above. Through the moments of daily life, the boy Giussani learned to be attentive to others and open to the world. As he walked through the town, "If my dad had not shaken my hand one thousand times to have me say 'Good morning,' I never would have learned to say 'Good morning' to people."[3] When his mother tucked him in at night, she used to say to her son, "Let us remember those who are poor … let us remember what happened in Japan, the war ongoing in China."[4]

It was in this family context that the priestly vocation matured in young Giussani. He entered the St Peter

Martyr seminary for the Diocese of Milan, in Seveso, in October of 1933. In 1937, he moved on to the expansive minor Venegono Seminary in Varese, where he continued his studies in preparation for the priesthood.

Under the tutelage of the professors at the "School of Venegono," Fr Giussani's vocational path was enriched by their solid foundation, which would bear fruit in all the later developments of his life and his mission as a priest. He later recalled, "Everything happened thanks to the faithfulness to the education I received [in his years in seminary, both in high school and the archdiocesan seminary at Venegono] from teachers who were real masters, who knew how to immerse me in a solid Christian tradition."[5] Throughout his life, Fr Giussani would point to the importance of their example for his growth in maturity in the faith. "If I had never encountered Msgr Gaetano Corti in high school, if I had never heard [...] Msgr Giovanni Colombo's Italian literature class, [...] Christ [...] would have been just a word that belonged in theological musings, or, in the best of cases, a reminder of a pietistic, but generic and foggy, sentimentality."[6]

In Venegono, teaching revolved around the centrality of the Incarnation, which fulfills man's every desire, and the discovery that faith is supremely reasonable, because it responds to the questions of the heart. One moment was decisive in the life of the young seminarian: "When I was thirteen, I memorized all of Leopardi's poems, because the questions he raised seemed to overshadow all other themes. For an entire month, I only studied Leopardi, [...] the most evocative travelling companion on my religious itinerary." He later would say, "I think I always remained faithful to my youthful decision to re-cite one of his poems to myself every day, having learned them all by heart in eighth grade."[7] Leopardi's poetry touched young Giussani's heart in a decisive way, re-vealing to him the full depth of the desire for the infinite that is in the heart of every human. Cardinal Ratzinger noted it when he celebrated Fr Giussani's funeral Mass: "From the start, he was touched, or better, wounded, by the desire for beauty. He was not satisfied with any beauty whatever, a banal beauty; he was looking rather for Beauty itself, infinite Beauty."[8]

Equally decisive was another event, which happened to Giussani at the beginning of high school, shortly after his "encounter" with Leopardi. "Everything came like the surprise of a 'beautiful day,' when a teacher in my first year of high school [his name was Fr Gaetano Corti] – I was 15 years old – read and explained the first page of the Gospel of John. At the time, the passage had to be read at the end of every Mass, so I had heard it thousands of times." But then came that "beautiful day" when his teacher explained the first page of the Gospel of John: "The Word of God, in other words, that of which all things are made, was made flesh," he said, "and so, beauty was made flesh, goodness was made flesh, justice was made flesh; love, life, and truth were made flesh. Being is not in a Platonic realm of ideas, it became flesh, and it is alive among us." "In that moment, I thought that Leopardi expressed, eighteen hundred years later, the begging for that event which had already happened, which St John announced."[9]

Cardinal Ratzinger would say of Giussani that, "he was looking rather for Beauty itself, infinite Beauty, and thus he found Christ, in Christ true beauty, the path of life, the true joy."[10]

That moment was a revolution for the young seminarian, as he himself would later attest. "My life was literally seized by this; both as a memory that my thoughts persistently returned to, and as the stimulus to reevaluate each aspect of everyday life. From that moment on, no instant was without meaning. Everything that existed, and so everything that was beautiful, true, attractive, or fascinating – even if only potentially so – had its foundation and meaning in that message, like the certainty of a presence in which lies a hope that embraces everything."[11]

Within the environment of Venegono, Giussani was formed as an authentically Ambrosian priest. In seminary, Giussani formed deep ties with a number of friends. Together, they formed what they called the *Studium Christi*, a small group that would "study" – in other words, seek out – Christ in all things, beginning with what they were learning in class. What they found was consistently documented in *Christus*, the newsletter that the group put out.

The young seminarians lived their youth and their path towards priesthood intensely. Giussani's life would be full of memories from those years. "One evening in the winter while at seminary, after dinner (when there was about an hour of free time), Enrico Manfredini and another of our friends, De Ponti [...], came up to me and said, 'Listen, if Christ is everything, what does He have to do with mathematics?' We were not yet sixteen years old. Everything in my life was born out of that question. That question channelled into an organic initiative all my life was able to give; my thoughts, sentiments, and effort. [...] It is as if all of our faith is concentrated and rests upon that question." Another memory from Venegono also involved Enrico. "While we were heading down to church [...], Manfredini said to me, 'Just think! God became a man, just like us ...' He stopped short, and it stuck with me, so much that I repeat it to you now, 'That God became man is something out of this world!' And I added, 'It's something out of this world, that lives *in* this world!,' and so the world is changed, is more livable. It becomes more beautiful."[12]

In March of 1945, the rector of Venegono, Msgr Petazzi, assigned Giussani to remain in seminary to continue his studies and to teach. He was ordained a priest at the hands of Cardinal Ildefonso Schuster in the Duomo of Milan on 26 May 1945. During the following months, he spent every Saturday and Sunday helping at the parish of Sts Nazaro and Celso, in the Barona neighbourhood in the suburbs of Milan. Soon after his ordination, he was struck with a respiratory illness and had to give up his work in the parish. The sickness would accompany him for the rest of his life. He later wrote to a friend from Varigotti, the seaside town where he was sent to recover, "Every moment that I spend in this forced inactivity, in the painful process of taking care of myself, can become a great act of love in service of the happiness of my fellow men and for the glory of my

Divine Friend, more than all my external zeal could have accomplished."[13]

Beginning in 1950, having regained his health, Fr Giussani began to help out on weekends at Sts Martino and Silvestro parish in Milan, on Viale Lazio. During his time in the confessional, he met students from local high schools and understood how difficult it was to live a Christian life at school, with teachers who constantly disparaged priests, religion, and the Church. The young people confessed not knowing how to respond to the objections posed. They were Catholics by tradition, but faith had not become a personal conviction. One particular confession changed Giussani's life.

He writes about the episode in his most famous book, *The Religious Sense*. In June of 1951, a teenage boy came to the church because his mother wanted him to go to confession before taking his exam to pass high school. The dialogue between the two went like this: The boy, who was named Luigi, said, "You cannot deny that the true grandeur of man is that of Dante's Capaneus, that giant chained by God in hell, yet who cries to God, 'I cannot free myself from these chains because you bind me here. You cannot, however, prevent me from blaspheming, and so I blaspheme you.' This is the true grandeur of man." A few moments went by and then Fr Giussani, rather than scolding him or lecturing him, posed a simple question to challenge the boy: "But isn't it even greater to love the infinite?" The teen left the church and Giussani didn't see him again until a few months later, when he appeared again and told the young priest, "for two weeks I've been receiving the sacraments because what you said has been 'eating away' at me all summer."[14]

Encounters such as these led Fr Giussani to think that perhaps the Lord didn't want him to be a theologian, but rather to work with young people to educate them in the faith. Based on his observations of young people, he became convinced that no one had ever taught them a method to verify if Christ and the faith could respond to the deepest needs of the human heart – the needs for truth, beauty, justice and happiness. As he underlines in his book *The Risk of Education*, all of Fr Giussani's efforts had the aim of "demonstrating the relevance of faith to answer life's needs." "Through my education at home and formation in seminary, and later through my own meditation, I was thoroughly persuaded that a faith that could not be found or confirmed in present experience, that was not useful to its needs, would not be a faith capable of standing up in a world in which everything, *everything*, says the opposite." For Giussani, "faith corresponds to the fundamental, original needs of the heart of every man and woman."[15] Giussani wanted to demonstrate this weight and importance of the Christian gospel to all those he met.

Pursuing this goal, in 1953 he began to participate as an advisor for *Gioventù Studentesca* [Student Youth], which was the branch of Catholic Action for high school students in Milan. In his time travelling on the train to Milan, he met even more young people who were ignorant of the tenets of the faith, which convinced him of the need to take action. He wrote of the urgency that slowly grew inside of him: "I need to put the 'Purgatory' of work in this world before the 'Paradise' of theology. I felt this as a real duty. How could you sit there contemplating being and essence, which is a wonderfully beautiful thing to do when people are settled, if my Christian brothers and sisters continue to live in ignorance and indifference?"[16]

The personalization of the faith to which Pope Francis constantly refers was a decisive question for Fr Giussani. The reason is simple: only a person who becomes certain that the path to respond to all of life's needs is found in Christ can live freely, without being suffocated or overcome by external circumstances. Such a person will live as a "new man," with the creativity that Jesus alone makes possible. He expressed the same message in front of the Pope and the whole Church in 1987, at the Synod on the Laity. "What is Christianity, if not the event of a new man who, by his very nature, becomes a new presence in the world? [...] Today's men and women await, perhaps subconsciously, an encounter with people for whom the fact of Christ is such a real presence that their lives are changed. What can reach today's man? The impact with a person; an event that is an echo of the first event, when Jesus looked up and said, 'Zacchaeus, come down quickly, I am coming to your house.'"[17]

With this urgency, Fr Giussani received permission from his superiors to teach religion at the Liceo Berchet, a prestigious high school in Milan, beginning in 1954. "I remember as if it were today: Berchet high school, nine o'clock in the morning, the first day of school in October of 1954. I remember the feeling I had as I climbed the few stairs at the entrance of the building. It was naive enthusiasm, a simple boldness that made me leave behind the life of teaching theology at the seminary at Venegono, which I loved, to help young people to rediscover the terms of authentic faith."[18]

In his classes, he spoke of the religious sense, the reasonableness of the faith, the fact of the Incarnation of Christ as the centre of reality and of human life, and of the Church as the place established by God to ensure the continual presence of Christ in history, up to the present. To this, he always added the invitation to students to verify the truth of what he said in their own lives, willing to risk what he said in the court of the freedom of his listeners. "I'm not here so that you can take my ideas as your own; I'm here to teach you a true method that you can use to judge the things I will tell you. And what I have to tell you is the result of a long experience, of a two-thousand-year-old history."[19]

From the mid-1950s on, there was always a group of young people who were fascinated by Giussani's vibrant way of presenting the truth of the Christian tradition. He taught about the faith by engaging students in a present experience, something that could be lived out, and in fact, something without which it was impossible to live fully.

It was the beginning of a "human adventure," a "movement" – first Gioventù Studentesca, and later Communion and Liberation – that would spread throughout Italy and around the world, not according to a strategic plan, but propelled by the force of witnesses, passing from one person to another. As Fr Giussani described it, "In 1954, all of a sudden, we came onto the scene at the public school. [...] We didn't begin trying to come up with an alternative scheme for the school; we went into it *with the awareness that we carried that which saves humanity at school and everywhere,* that makes life fully human and makes our search for truth authentic: *Christ present in our unity.*" This is the method that Fr Giussani always followed, full of certainty that it is the Lord who accomplishes all things. "Our last thought was the next week that would come, or if we would still even be there."[20]

All of Fr Giussani's life can be summed up in a phrase that he wrote to a friend in 1946, in a period of recovery from the illness that had struck him just a year after his priestly ordination. He wrote, "The greatest joy in a man's life is to feel Christ alive and beating in his heart, taking flesh in his thoughts. All else is rubbish or fleeting illusion."[21] This is the motivation behind his passion for education and his urgent desire to communicate the full truth and beauty of the resurrected Christ in an "act of love for the souls of my many brothers and sisters in humanity, for whose happiness the Lord Jesus died; for whose eternal happiness the Lord Jesus called me to give my life along with His...[...] It's been many years since I have cried except for two reasons: because of the thought of the eternal unhappiness of my fellow men, and the thought of the earthly unhappiness of men and women, which is a symbol of the eternal one. Jesus has chosen us to proclaim His Love and human happiness to all the world; to proclaim the great and inexpressible happiness that awaits us."[22] Pope John Paul II would say the same in 2002, underlining how Fr Giussani would have "wanted and wants not to indicate *a* road, but *the* road to arrive at the resolution of the existential drama in life. The road, as you [Fr Giussani] have affirmed so many times, is Christ."[23]

This experience of familiarity with Christ is what allowed Fr Giussani to become a father to many young people and adults who, thanks to his witness, were able to encounter Christ as an attractive and living Presence. As Cardinal Ratzinger underlined, "Monsignor Giussani, with his unabashed and unfailing faith knew that [...] Christ, and the encounter with Him, is always at the centre because he who does not give God gives too little."[24] Pope Francis continuously reminds us of the same point, witnessing to us what is essential to live the faith of the Church. "I invite all Christians, everywhere, at this very moment, to a renewed personal encounter with Jesus Christ, or at least openness to letting him encounter them; I ask all of you to do this unfailingly each day."[25] As Fr Giussani said in St Peter's Square in an audience with John Paul II on 30 May 1998, "The real protagonist of history is the beggar: Christ who begs for man's heart, and man's heart that begs for Christ."[26]

With his life, Fr Giussani showed us all what can happen to a man who lets himself be seized by Christ, therefore showing us the task of all the baptized: to give a grateful witness to Him who animates man's inner being. For him, "the Mystery of the Church, which has been handed on to us from 2000 years ago, must always 'happen again' through grace. It must always be a presence that moves, a movement that, by its nature, makes life in the place around it more human. The encounter with the redemptive event of Christ is always accompanied by the liberation of one's full humanity. 'Whoever follows me will have eternal life, and the hundred-fold here on earth.'"[27] This is the significance of faith in human life, not only for the life to come, but here and now.

During a presentation of the Spanish edition of *The Religious Sense* in 1998, then-Archbishop of Buenos Aires Jorge Mario Bergoglio said that "for many years now, [Giussani's] writings have inspired me to reflect and have helped me to pray. They have taught me to be a better Christian, and I am here presenting today to bear witness to this. Msgr Giussani is one of those unexpected gifts the Lord gave to our Church after Vatican II. He has caused a wealth of individuals and movements to rise up outside of pastoral structures and programs, movements that are offering miracles of new life within the Church."[28] With these words, the future Pope Francis described an experience that was shared by thousands of people in Italy and around the world, and that continues to occur now after the death of Fr Giussani. Countless individuals, despite never having met him, attribute much to their personal "encounter" with him through his books or by meeting some of his many spiritual sons and daughters.

People from all over the spectrum of religious or cultural backgrounds speak of Fr Giussani as a close friend, as a companion on the journey who shows the possibility of living the faith – and therefore living the fullness of humanity – in ordinary circumstances: in family life, at work, or in school. In him they find a credible witness along the path to holiness to which all who are baptized are called in their faithfulness to Church tradition. As he once said, "The real miracle is humanity lived out in daily life, without great fanfare or exceptional circumstances, it doesn't require luck; it's in eating, drinking, waking up and going to sleep overtaken by the awareness of a Presence, which has as its vehicles hands to be touched, faces that we see, forgiveness to be given, money to be distributed, and in a task to be completed, work that we're asked to say yes to."[29]

This is the promise of Christ – and it is a fulfilled promise, not an empty one – that Fr Giussani gave his life to proclaim. "In the simplicity of my heart, I have gladly given you everything."[30]

Julián Carrón
President of Fraternity of Communion and Liberation

1 The Religious Sense

"HOW THE ULTIMATE QUESTIONS ARISE"
The Religious Sense (Montreal & Kingston: McGill-Queen's University Press, 1997), 100–1

With this excerpt, taken from his most famous book, Fr Giussani describes the inner workings of the religious sense. The fundamental needs that are at the heart of all human experience – the need for truth, beauty, goodness, justice, and happiness – are awakened in each man and woman as they engage with reality, which generates the wonder of things as "presences."

Picture yourself being born, coming out of your mother's womb at the age you are now at this very moment in terms of your development and consciousness. What would be the first, absolutely your initial reaction? If I were to open my eyes for the first time in this instant, emerging from my mother's womb, I would be overpowered by the wonder and awe of things as a "presence." I would be bowled over and amazed by the stupefying repercussion of a presence which is expressed in current language by the word "thing." Things! That's "something!" "Thing," which is a concrete and, if you please, banal version of the word "being." *Being:* not as some abstract entity, but as presence, a presence which I do not myself make, which I find. A presence which imposes itself upon me.

He who does not believe in God is inexcusable, says St Paul in his letter to the Romans (Rom 1:19–21), because that person must deny this original phenomenon, this original experience of the "other." A baby lives this experience without being aware of it, because he is not yet completely conscious. But the adult who does not live it or does not consciously perceive it, is less than a baby. That person is atrophied.

The awe, the marvel of this reality which imposes itself upon me, of this presence which reaches me, is at the origin of the awakening of human consciousness. "Radical amazement is to the understanding of the realness of God what clarity and distinctness are to the comprehension of mathematical ideas ... Devoid of wonder, we remain deaf to the sublime."[1]

Therefore, the very first sense of the human being is that of facing a reality which is not his, which exists independently of him, and upon which he depends. Empirically translated, it is the original perception of a *given*, a word which, if used in a completely human sense, involving the total person, all of the factors of an individual's personality, comes alive: "given," as a past participle, implies something which "gives." The word which translates in the content of human terms the word "given," and thus describes the content of our first impact with reality, is the word *gift*. But without dwelling on this, the very word "given" is also vibrant with an activity, in front of which I am passive: and it is a passivity which makes up my original activity of receiving, taking note, recognizing.

One time, while I was teaching in a high school, I asked: "So then, according to you, what does 'evidence' mean? Can one of you define it?" One boy, to the right of my chair, after a very long and embarrassed silence on the part of the students, exclaimed: "But then evidence is an inexorable presence!" Becoming aware of an inexorable presence! I open my eyes to this reality which imposes itself upon me, which does not depend upon me, but upon which I depend; it is the great conditioning of my existence – if you like, the given. It is this awe which awakens the ultimate question within us: not as a cold observation, but as a wonder pregnant with an attraction, almost a passivity in which simultaneously is conceived an attraction.

"I AM 'YOU-WHO-MAKE-ME'"
The Religious Sense, 105–6

We move from the wonder at the presence of the things in reality to the realization that man does not make himself; we are not making ourselves right now. It is the moving surprise at discovering one's "I," one's self, as dependent on the Mystery who makes all things: "I am 'You–who–make–me.'" The awakening awareness that God is more myself than I am; He is the ultimate meaning of my existence.

At this point, when an individual is reawakened within his being by the presence, the attraction, the awe, he is grateful, joyful, because this presence can be beneficial and providential. The human being becomes aware of himself as *I*, recovers this original awe with a depth that establishes the measure, the stature of his identity. At this moment, if I am attentive, that is, if I am mature, then I cannot deny that the greatest and most profound evidence is that *I do not make myself*, I am not making myself. I do not give myself being, or the reality which I am. I am "given." This is the moment of maturity when I discover myself to be dependent upon something else.

If I descend to my very depths, where do I spring from? Not from myself: from *something else*. This is the perception of myself as a gushing stream born from a spring, from something else, more than me, and by which I am made. If a stream rushing forth from a spring could think, it would perceive, at the bottom of its fresh surging, an origin it does not know, which is other than itself.

Here we are speaking of the intuition, which, in every period of history, the more intelligent human spirits have had. It is an intuition of this mysterious presence, which endows the instant, the "I" with substance (solidity, density, foundation). *I am you-who-make-me* — except that this *you* is absolutely faceless. I use this word *you* because it is the least inadequate in my experience as a human being to indicate that unknown presence which is beyond comparison, more than my experience as a human being. What other word could I, on the other hand, use? When I examine myself and notice that I am not making myself by myself, then I — with the full and conscious vibration of affection which this word I exudes – turn to the Thing that makes me, to the source that causes me to be in this instant, and I can only address it using the word *you*. *You-who-make-me* is, therefore, what religious tradition calls God – it is that which is more than I, more "I" than I myself. It is that by means of which I am.

For this reason, the Bible says of God: "tam pater nemo" (Gal. 4:6), or, no one is as much a father, because, in our experience, a father gives life its beginning which, from the first fraction of the first instant of being, detaches itself and goes off on its own. A woman expressed this to me in a most surprising way. When I was still a very young priest, this woman would come regularly for confession. For some time I did not see her anymore, and, when she returned, she said to me: "I had a second baby girl." Before I could reply, she added: "I was truly surprised! Just as I became aware that she had been born, I did not think of whether it was a boy or a girl, whether it was healthy or not. No, the first idea that came to mind was this: 'Look here, it is starting to go on its own.'"

Whereas God, Father in every instant, is conceiving me *now*. No one is so much a father: he who generates.

To be conscious of oneself right to the core is to perceive, at the depths of the self, an Other. This is prayer: to be conscious of oneself to the very centre, to the point of meeting an Other. Thus prayer is the only human gesture which totally realizes the human being's stature.

The "I," the human being, is that level of nature in which nature becomes aware of not being made by itself. In this way, the entire cosmos is like the continuation of my body. But one could also say that the human being is that level of nature in which nature experiences its own *contingency*. Man experiences himself as contingent, subsists by means of something else, because he does not make himself by himself. I stand on my feet because I lean on another. I am because I am made. Like my voice, which is the echo of a vibration, if I cease the vibration, it no longer exists. Like spring water rising up – it is, in its entirety, derived from its source. And like a flower which depends completely upon the support of its roots.

"TO LIVE THE REAL INTENSELY"
The Religious Sense, 108–9

There is just one condition to live in an authentically religious way: "to live always the real intensely without preclusion, without negating or forgetting anything." The human heart attains greatness precisely in facing daily circumstances, whatever they might be, because they are all signs of the Mystery.

What is the formula for the journey to the ultimate meaning of reality? Living the real. There is an experience, hidden yet implied, of that arcane, mysterious presence to be found within the opening of the eye, within the attraction reawakened by things, within the beauty of things, within an amazement, full of gratitude, comfort, and hope. And this is so because these things move themselves in such a way that they serve me, are useful to me. Numbered among these things is myself as well – myself, in whom that presence which is concealed, hidden, becomes close, because it is here, forming me but also informing me of good and evil.

Now the question is this: How can this complex, yet simple, this enormously rich experience of the human heart – which is the heart of the human person and, therefore, of nature, the cosmos – how can it become vivid, how can it come alive? How can it become powerful? In the *"impact" with the real*. The only condition for being truly and faithfully religious, the formula for the journey to the meaning of reality is to always live the real intensely, without preclusion, without negating or forgetting anything. Indeed, it would not be human, that is to say, reasonable, to take our experience at face value, to limit it to just the crest of the wave, without going down to the core of its motion.

The positivism that dominates modern man excludes the call emanating from our original relationship with things, to search for meaning. This relationship invites us to seek substance, a meaning, and enables us to sense this presence that provides substance which things themselves are not. This is so true that I (and it is here that the problem is defined), I myself am not this presence either, because I am the level where the stars and the earth become aware of their own lack of substance. Positivism excludes the invitation to discover the meaning addressed to us precisely by our original and immediate impact with reality. It would have us accept appearances. And this is suffocating.

The more one lives this level of consciousness in his relationship with things, the more intense the impact with reality, and the more one begins to know mystery.

Let us repeat: a trivial relationship with reality, whose most symptomatic aspect is preconception, blocks the authentic religious dimension, the true religious fact. The mark of great souls and persons who are truly alive is an eagerness for this search, carried out through their commitment to the reality of their existence.

Here then is the conclusion: we could say that the world, this reality into which we collide unleashes a word, an invitation, a meaning as if upon impact. The world is like a word, a "logos" which sends you further, calls you on to another, beyond itself, further up. In Greek "up" is expressed with the word *ana*. This is the value of *analogy*: the structure of the "impact" of the human being with reality awakens within the individual a voice which draws him towards a meaning which is further on, further up – *ana*.

Analogy: this word sums up the dynamic structure of the human being's "impact" with reality.

2 Traces of the Christian Experience

THE FORMULATION OF THE HUMAN PROBLEM
The Journey to Truth Is an Experience (Montreal &
Kingston: McGill-Queen's University Press, 2006), 53–7

In order to recognize the response to what the religious sense awaits, we have to seriously formulate our own experience of the "human" problem and resulting questions. We must begin by looking at our own experience to the point of understanding the depth of our original needs, which, according to Christ, are a promise fulfilled in His person. In this short text, which is one of his first, Fr Giussani summarizes the methodical components of his Christian proposal, one that took form within the great tradition of the Church and was developed to help to show how she is an ever-present event. Christ reveals Himself as the "catalyst" in human life and the sure road to a more fully human life. He refers to "the essence of the Christian fact as the proposal of a life. This is just how we began: speaking of Christ."

Even after sharing their lives with Jesus for such a long time, after the disaster of Calvary and the mystery of Easter, after all that, the Apostles understood little of Him. Only a few hours before His ascent into Heaven, they still asked Him when He would establish the Kingdom of Israel, such as everyone conceived it at that time: a kingdom of earthly and political power.

If they did not understand Him, why did they follow Him? And among them were those who had left wife, children, home, boat and nets, offices, business. Why did they follow Him?

They followed Christ because he had become the focus of their affections. Why?

Where they were unaware and confused, they were enlightened, for Christ was the only one in whose words they felt their whole human experience understood and their needs taken seriously, clarified. Thus, for instance, those very people who used to believe that their only need was bread began to understand that "Man does not live by bread alone."

Christ introduces Himself to them in just this way, as *an Other*, who surprisingly moves in their direction, helps them, explains their troubles to them; He cures them if they are crippled or blind, heals their souls, responds to their needs, is within their experience. But what are their experiences? Their experiences, their needs are their very selves, those men and women, their own human nature.

Thus Christ is right here, in my attitude and disposition as a human being, in my way, that is, as one who expects, awaits something because I sense that I am entirely wanting. He has joined me. He has proposed Himself to my original needs.

Hence, to meet Christ we must first formulate our human problem seriously.

First, we must open ourselves to ourselves. In other words, we must be acutely aware of our experiences, look on the humanity within us with sympathy; we must take into consideration who we really are. To take into consideration means to take seriously what we experience, *everything* we experience, to discover every aspect, to seek the complete meaning.

We must be very careful, because all too easily we do not start from our true experience; that is, from our experience in its entirety and authenticity. We often identify our experience with partial impressions, truncating it, as often happens with affective matters, when we fall in love or dream about the future.

Even more often we confuse our experience with the prejudices or schemes that we absorb from our environment, perhaps unaware. Therefore, instead of opening up to that attitude of expectation, sincere attention, and dependence that our experience suggests and fervently demands, we impose categories and explanations that constrict and distress our experience, while presuming to resolve it.

The myth that "scientific progress one day will solve all our needs" is the modern formula of this presumption, a wild and repugnant presumption, because it does not consider or even know our real needs. It refuses to observe our experience clearly and to accept what it means to be human, with all the needs that this implies. For this reason modern civilization causes us to move blindly between this exasperated presumption and darkest despair.

Solitude

A vital cue comes to us from the situation of the Apostles as narrated to us in verses 9 to 11 in the first chapter of the Acts.

Christ has left and they remain there still and astonished. Hope has vanished and solitude falls upon them just as darkness and cold descend on the earth after sunset. The more we discover our needs, the more we become aware that we cannot resolve them on our own. Nor can others, people like us. A sense of *powerlessness* accompanies every serious experience in our lives.

This sense of powerlessness generates *solitude*. True solitude does not come from being physically alone but from the discovery that a fundamental problem of ours cannot find its solution in us or in others.

We can well say that the sense of solitude is born in the very heart of every serious commitment to our own humanity. Those who believe they have found the solution to a great need of theirs in something or someone, only to have this something or someone disappear or prove incapable of resolving this need, can understand this. We are alone in our needs, in our need to be and to live intensely, like one alone in the desert. All he or she can do is wait until someone appears. And human persons will certainly not provide the solution because it is precisely their needs that must be resolved.

Community

The apostles returned to the place where Christ had ascended into heaven and they stayed together (Acts 1:12–14).

One who truly discovers and lives the experience of powerlessness and solitude does not remain alone. Only one who has experienced powerlessness to his depths, and hence personal solitude, feels close to others and is easily drawn to them. Like someone lost, without shelter in a storm, he or she feels his cry at one with the cries of others, his or her anxiety and expectation at one with the anxieties and expectations of all others.

Only one who truly experiences helplessness and solitude stays with other people without self-interest, calculation, or imposition, yet at the same time without "following the crowd" passively, submitting or becoming a slave of society. You can claim to be seriously committed to your own human experience only when you sense this community with others, with anyone and everyone, without frontiers and discrimination, for we live our commitment to what is most deeply within us and therefore common to all. You are truly committed to your own human experience when, saying "I," you live this "I" so simply and profoundly that you feel fraternally bonded to any other person's "I." God's answer will reach only the person committed in such a way.

It must immediately be pointed out that this solidarity with all of humanity is achieved in a particular place. Even in the Acts (see 1:13, 23–6), the community of the apostles is born in a very specific situation. They did not choose the place or the people. They found themselves there almost by chance and their whole life depended on this fact.

This is how our personal humanity is born, shaped, and nourished, in a particular *setting*: we find ourselves in it, we don't choose it.

Our effort to understand the entire setting and offer our sense of community to all the people in that setting, measures the openness of our human commitment and is commensurate with the sincerity of our commitment to all humanity. It is not up to us to exclude anyone from the experience of our human life; only God can make that choice and He does so through the situation in which He places us. Otherwise it would be a private matter on our part, a selfish looking-inward; we would be taking advantage of a given situation through our own preconceived schemes.

Authority

Peter, the most representative person in the community, stands up and speaks, and he is heeded (see Acts 1:15–22).

In our particular milieu some individuals have a greater sensitivity to the human experience; *in fact* they develop a deeper understanding of any given situation and of others; *in fact* they are more likely to influence the movement that builds a community. They live our experience more intensely and with a greater commitment. We all feel that they are more representative of us. With them we feel closer to, and stay more willingly in community with, others. To acknowledge this phenomenon is to be loyal to one's own humanity, a duty spurred by wisdom.

When we discover ourselves helpless and alone, our humanity spurs us to come together. If we meet someone who better feels and understands our experience, suffering, needs, and expectations, we naturally are led to follow that person and become his or her disciple. In that sense, such persons naturally constitute *authority* for us even if they do not carry special rights or titles. Naturally, above all, it is one who most loyally lives or understands the human experience who becomes an authority.

Thus authority is born as a wealth of experience that imposes itself on others. It generates freshness, wonder, and respect. Inevitably, it is attractive; it is evocative. Not to value the presence of this *effective authority* that His Being places in every setting is to cling pettily to our own limits. The Jews said of Christ: "This is one who has authority" and they abandoned the schemes of the Pharisees to follow Him.

The encounter with this natural authority develops our sensitivity and our conscience; it helps us to better discover our nature and what we aspire to from the depths of our present poverty.

3   At the Origin of the Christian Claim

THE ENIGMA AS A FACT WITHIN THE HUMAN
TRAJECTORY
At the Origin of the Christian Claim (Montreal & Kingston:
McGill-Queen's University Press, 1999), 29–33, 34

In this chapter, Fr Giussani describes the passage from the religious sense to the event of Jesus Christ. All of man's religious attempts throughout the ages reached the same conclusion, that it was impossible to give a name and face to the Mystery. This gave rise to the hypothesis of revelation, that God Himself might come to assist. At a set place and time in history, Jesus of Nazareth not only revealed the Mystery, but also identified Himself with God.

Man's demand for revelation sums up the condition of his spirit in conceiving of and realizing the relationship with the divine according to the alternative that this diagram expresses.

The horizontal line represents the trajectory of human history, above which looms the presence of an X: destiny, fate, the ultimate something, mystery, "God."

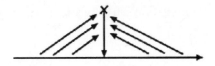

Throughout the trajectory of history, in theoretical and practical terms, humanity has sought to comprehend the relationship binding its contingent reality, its ephemeral point, and its ultimate meaning, to imagine and live the link between his own transitory nature and the eternal. Let us suppose that the enigma of x, the enigmatic presence looming beyond the horizon (without which reason could not be reason, because reason is the affirmation of the ultimate meaning) were to penetrate the fabric of history, join in the flow of time and space and, with an unimaginable expressive force, become a "Fact" incarnate in our midst. But, in this hypothesis, what does "incarnate" mean? It means to assume that the mysterious x became a phenomenon, a regular fact that could act upon and be registered in the trajectory of history.

This supposition would correspond to the need for revelation. It would be irrational to exclude the possibility that the mystery, which makes all things, could reach the point where it becomes directly and personally involved with man in the trajectory of history. For we have already seen how, by our very nature, we cannot prescribe the boundaries of mystery.

Therefore, given the possibility of the fact and the rationality of the hypothesis, what is left for us to do when confronted with it? We can only ask ourselves: *did it or did it not happen?* [...]

A Radical Overturning of the Religious Method

The hypothesis that the mystery has penetrated man's existence by speaking to him in human terms alters the man-destiny relationship which will no longer be based on human effort, the fruit of man's construction or imagination, the study of a distant, enigmatic thing, or on waiting for something absent. Instead, it will mean coming up against something present. If God had manifested a particular will in a particular way in human history, if he had charted a pathway of his own leading us to him, the central issue of the religious phenomenon would cease to be man attempting to imagine God, even though this attempt is the greatest expression of human dignity. Instead, the whole issue would lie in freedom's pure and simple gesture of acceptance or rejection.

This is the overturning of the method. No longer is the focal point the striving of the intelligence, the drive of the will to construct, the stretching of the imagination, the weaving of a complex moralism. Rather, it is simple recognition, the reaction of one who, watching out for the arrival of a friend, singles him out of the crowd and greets him. In this hypothesis, the religious method would lose all of its disturbing connotations of an enigmatic deferment to something in the distance. Rather, it would have the dynamics of an experience, the experience of a present, an encounter.

It should be noted that the first method favours the intelligent man, the cultured, the fortunate, the powerful, while the second favours the poor, the ordinary man. To encounter a person who is present is as easy for a child to grasp as an adult. In this hypothesis, the dynamics of revelation would cease to primarily emphasize ingeniousness and initiative, but would stress simplicity and love. Love, in fact, represents man's only true dependence, the affirmation of the Other as our very substance, the supreme choice of freedom. But under such an hypothesis, it would no longer be presumptuous to affirm only one pathway. It would be obedience to a fact, the decisive Fact of all time.

One way to escape remains – to deny that this Fact is possible at all. Such a crime against the supreme category of reason, of possibility, was condemned by Graham Greene's priest in the face of the crazed hate of a "free thinker." In *The End of the Affair* the priest demonstrated hatred's profound contradiction by saying that it seemed more like free thinking to admit all possibilities rather than to preclude some of them.[1]

No Longer Just an Hypothesis

We have seen that this hypothesis is possible and, if true, would revolutionize the religious method. We must now recognize that it was and is believed to be true in the history of man. The Christian message says: "Yes, this happened."

Let us picture the world as an immense plain where numerous groups of human beings, under the direction of engineers and architects, are busy working on disparate projects to build bridges with thousands of arches serving as links between earth and heaven, between the ephemeral place of their existence and the "star" of destiny. With its infinite number of building sites the plain is a hive of activity. At a certain point a man arrives on the scene, and his gaze embraces the whole frenzied workplace. Suddenly, he shouts: "Stop!" Those closest to him cease working, and then gradually the others follow until they are all watching him. And he tells them: "You are great and noble. You are making a sublime effort, but it is an unhappy one because you will never manage to build a road linking your world with the ultimate mystery. Abandon your projects, lay down your tools. Destiny has taken pity on you. Follow me and I will build the bridge, for *I* am destiny." Now let us try to imagine the reaction of all those people to such a declaration. First the architects, then the work foremen, then the best of the artisans would find themselves telling their labourers instinctively: "Don't stop working. Keep going. Can't you see this man is crazy?" And they would echo: "Of course, he must be crazy." Resuming their work on their bosses' orders, others might say: "You can see he's crazy." There would be just a few who would not take their eyes off this man, for they have been profoundly moved. They would not obey their bosses as the masses had done, but would approach and follow him.

Within this flight of fancy is the story of what happened in history and is still happening now.

At this point, we no longer find ourselves confronting a theoretical (philosophical or moral) problem, but an historical one. The first question we must ask is not: "Is what the Christian message says reasonable or right?" but "Did it happen or not?" or "Did God really intervene in history?"

Although implied in our earlier discussion, I would like to stress that this "new" question requires a different method, which could be explained like this: man may, indeed must, arrive at the discovery of the existence of a mysterious something, of God, through his analytical perception of his own experience of reality (and we have seen how ample historical documentation demonstrates that man normally reaches this discovery in this way); the issue now, since it is a question of an historical fact, cannot be verified by analytical reflection on the structure of one's own relationship with reality. It is a fact that either happened in history or did not: it either exists or it does not, it either transpired or did not. It was either a real event which emerged in man's existence as part of history and therefore must be recognized as an event, or it remains just a notion. Faced with this hypothesis, the method is the historical registration of an objective fact.

Then, the question: "Did God really intervene in history?" must refer, above all, to that incomparable claim which is the content of a precise message. It must necessarily become another question: "Who is Jesus?" Christianity arises as the answer to this question.

[...]

The Christian imperative is that the content of its message presents itself as a fact. This cannot be stressed enough.

An insidious cultural disloyalty, aided by the ambiguity and fragility of Christians as well, has facilitated the dissemination of a vague notion of Christianity as a discourse or doctrine and perhaps, therefore, a fable or moral. No. First and foremost it is a fact – a man joined the ranks of men.

But the imperative embraces another aspect of the fact: the advent of that man is an announcement transmitted down through the years to us today. To this very day, this event has been proclaimed and announced as the event of a Presence. That one man said: "I am God," and that this is passed on as a present fact, forcefully demands a personal stance. We can smile about it or decide not to bother with it: this would mean, in any case, that we decided to resolve the problem in a negative way, that we have not wanted to face up to a proposal whose dimensions are so great that they are beyond the realms of human imagination.

This is why society so often turns away from this announcement and wishes to confine it to churches and individual conscience. What society finds most disturbing is the vastness of the dimensions of the problem: whether he did or did not exist, or rather, whether *he does exist* or *existed*; whether we can verify it or not; this is the greatest decision of our existence. No other choice that society could propose or man could imagine as important has this value. And it sounds like an imposition. The affirmation of the Christian message appears to be despotism. But is announcing the news of something that happened, however great, really despotism?

4   Why the Church?

HOW TO ENTER INTO AN UNDERSTANDING
OF THE CHURCH
Why the Church? (Montreal & Kingston: McGill-Queen's
University Press, 2001), 5–6, 7–9

*How can we, who live 2,000 years after the events narrated in the
Gospels, know with certainty if what Christ proclaims is significant for our life now? In this chapter, Fr Giussani aims to
demonstrate how the Church is an historical phenomenon whose
only meaning lies in the fact that it enables contemporary man to
attain a certainty about Christ. Christ remains present in history through the companionship of those who believe in Him.*

A Fundamental Presupposition

The Church is not just an expression of life, something born
from life. It *is* a life, a life which has come down to us
through many centuries. Anyone seeking to verify a personal opinion of the Church must keep in mind that any real
understanding of a life, which is the Church, requires that
one share that life in a way that lets him or her know it.

Although true understanding of a reality which is somehow bound to life demands time, it is difficult to calculate just how much. In a reality which arises from life, there are characteristics and aspects we never cease to discover and fathom.

The *conditio sine qua non* for understanding life is *living out a shared existence* with it. Normally, an individual is tempted to set a limit, either a pre-established one upon which, at a certain point, he decides. To avoid the limitations this implies requires a particular position of simplicity and loyalty. Otherwise, a person will restrict the possibility of making a critical judgment about this form of life and concomitantly, make even a minimum of objectivity impossible.

Being in Tune with the Phenomenon

Whatever the position of an individual approaching the Church, it is a reality which can be categorized among religious phenomena. Some might judge it as a falsified, or falsifying religious phenomenon of little interest, while others might take its validity for granted. But in no case, I believe, can we avoid categorizing it as a religious reality. It is precisely this point that I propose we consider first of all.

The Church is religious "life." [...]

Training the Focus on the Originality of Christianity

This theme of the religious sense is important for an understanding of the originality of Christianity, which is nothing more than the answer, through Christ and the Church, to our religious sense. Christianity is a solution to the religious problem, and while *not* the means of resolving political, social, and economic problems, the Church is the instrument of this solution.

The gravest errors along all of man's pathways have their origins rooted in the religious sense. And since we have reached the final volume in this trilogy I want to return to the point of departure in our reflection, which, if left undeveloped, becomes a hindrance to every step of the way. If it is developed, however, it becomes the irreplaceable yeast needed for the reasonable progression of the human spirit. […]

The Heart of the Church Problem

How can those who encounter Jesus Christ a day, a month, a hundred, a thousand, or two thousand years after his disappearance from earthly horizons, be enabled to realize that he corresponds to the truth which he claims? In other words, how does one come to see whether Jesus of Nazareth is or is not in a strict sense that event which incarnates the hypothesis of revelation?

This problem is the heart of what history has always called Church.

The word "Church" indicates an historical phenomenon whose only meaning lies in the fact that it enables man to attain a certainty about Christ. It is, in short, the answer to this question: "How can I, who arrived the day after Christ left, know that this really is Something of supreme interest to me, and how can I know this with any reasonable degree of certainty?" We have already noted[1] that, whatever the answer may be, it is impossible to imagine a problem graver than this for a human being. For any person who comes into contact with the Christian message, it is imperative that he or she attempt to obtain a certainty about it, since this is such a decisive issue for his or her life and for the life of the world. The problem can obviously be censored, but considering the nature of the question, that would be like saying "no."

It is important, therefore, that he who comes after the event of Jesus of Nazareth – a long time after – may draw near to him today in such a way as to arrive at a reasonable and certain evaluation befitting the seriousness of the problem. The Church presents itself as the answer to this need for a sure evaluation. This is the theme we are about to deal with. Facing it head on presupposes the seriousness of the question: "In truth, who is Christ?" That is, not only does it presuppose that we make a moral commitment by putting our conscience to work in the face of the historical fact of the Christian message, ultimately it also assumes a moral seriousness in the life of the religious sense as such.

If, on the contrary, we do not make a commitment to that inevitable and omnipresent aspect of life which is the religious sense, if we think that we have the option not to assume a personal position concerning the historical fact of Christ, then the interest that the Church has for our lives will only be reduced to the level of sociological or political problem, or a problem of association to be fought for or defended according to these various points of view. But how degrading for reason to be stripped of an authentic and living religious sense, the one aspect that makes its connective capacity more human and fulfilled! However, it is a fact that, whether we like it or not, whether we resist or come to terms with it, the annunciation of God made man runs right through the entire course of history.

"THROUGH HUMAN REALITY"
Why the Church? (Montreal & Kingston: McGill-Queen's University Press, 2001), 72–3, 123–8

The Church makes divine realities present through the human-ity of those who are seized by Christ, transformed through Bap-tism. It was this same claim made by Jesus that scandalized the scribes and the Pharisees: that God, to respond to the urgencies of life, would choose to be incarnated in a man who walks, talks, and eats as they did.

The first nucleus of the Church demonstrated that it "not only carries on his work (Christ's), but she is his very continuation, in a sense far more real than that in which it can be said that any human institution is its founder's continuation." The Church then, even at the beginning, showed us that in its bond with Jesus [...] "she really makes him present."[1] [...]

Try then to imagine the scene: it is around the Paschal season, when Jews throughout the world would be in-tent, as far as possible, on travelling to Jerusalem as pil-grims. Try also to imagine the reactions of one of these pilgrims, who, on going to the temple for a few days in a row, would have noticed, each time, a little group of people under the portico. The first day he would have proceeded on his way, without wondering why, and on the second day, he might have done the same. But at some point, he certainly would have asked someone, "Who are those people I always see together here?" And they would have replied: "They are the followers of Jesus of Nazareth." And so we can see how the Church began: it literally allowed itself to "be seen" under Solomon's Portico [...].

The Church's most specific claim is not just that it is the vehicle of the divine, but that this vehicle works through human reality. Indeed, this is Christ's own claim. It was an insurmountable objection to the religious leaders and the educated people of his time, and it caused great scandal: "Is he not the carpenter, the son of Joseph?" (cf. Luke 4:22). "Surely he is one of us," they said, "one whose background we can trace, whose identity we can check, as we can anyone else's." Moreover, the height of the scandal was the fact that not only did his identity present nothing mysterious at first – he was a carpenter, the son of Joseph – but that his human personality displayed a disconcerting openness towards all sectors of the population. He did not hold back from the most unworthy of them, the lowest of the low, those most open to criticism. On the contrary, he clearly leaned towards them: "Why does he eat with tax collectors and sinners?" (Mark 2:16b). And such a man dared to say: "I am the way, the truth and the life. No one can come to the Father except through me" (John 14:6), daring to involve God with his own person to the extent of identifying himself with him.

And this is the scandal which the Church, in its essence and its existence in history, reproposes today and forever.

Through Human Reality

We have seen that what characterizes the Christian mystery is the revelation of the fact that God communicates himself to humanity through man, through human life.

To illustrate and support this, I would like to quote a few passages from the New Testament.

The following passage, from Paul's letter to the faithful in Thessalonica, in which he expresses his satisfaction at this community's response to his message, is significant: "Another reason why we continually thank God for you is that as soon as you heard the word that we brought you as God's message, you welcomed it for what it really is, not the word of any human being, but God's word, a power that is working among you believers" (1 Thess 2:13). Here, Paul is giving a very clear description of the phenomenon: the divine word which communicates itself through the voice of a man, the word of God brought by a man and accepted for what it really is, the word of the living God, active and creative in the lives of men.

As noteworthy is another of Paul's letters, where he is careful to underline that this word is so human a vehicle that it can even appear totally devoid of attraction, lacking the slightest wit. "Now when I came to you, brothers," the apostle admits, "I did not come with any brilliance of oratory or wise argument to announce to you the mystery of God … I came among you in weakness, in fear and great trembling and what I spoke and proclaimed was not meant to convince by philosophical argument; but to demonstrate the convincing power of the Spirit, so that your faith should depend not on human wisdom but on the power of God" (I Cor 2:1, 3–5).

And the letter he wrote to the Christians of Ephesus, attributed to his first period of imprisonment in Rome, reiterated a similar notion: "I, who am less than the least of all God's holy people, have been entrusted with this special grace, of proclaiming to the gentiles the unfathomable treasure of Christ and of throwing light on the inner workings of the mystery kept hidden through all the ages in God, the Creator of everything" (Eph 3:8–9).

Paul, then, was perfectly conscious of the innate disproportion in the phenomenon of the Church. By bringing its message through the vehicle of human reality, it is, therefore exposed to all the individual instances of human wretchedness, including his own. […]

Paul's awareness of disproportion becomes more acute in the ensuing moving passage in which he outlines some aspects of the lives of the evangelists at the time of the first communities: "For it seems to me that God has put us apostles on show right at the end, like men condemned to death: we have been exhibited as a spectacle to the whole universe, both angelic and human. Here we are, fools for Christ's sake, while you are the clever ones in Christ; we are weak, while you are strong; you are honoured, while we are disgraced. To this day, we go short of food and drink and clothes, we are beaten up and we have no homes; we earn our living by labouring with our own hands; when we are cursed we answer with a blessing; when we are hounded, we endure it passively; when we are insulted, we give a courteous answer. We are treated even now as the dregs of the world, the very lowest scum" (I Cor 4:9–13).

And yet these same apostles, Paul continues, "let light shine out of darkness, that has shone into our hearts to enlighten them with the knowledge of God's glory, the glory on the face of Christ," for "we hold this treasure in pots of earthenware, so that the immensity of the power is God's and not our own. We are subjected to every kind of hardship, but never distressed; we see no way out but we never despair; we are pursued but never cut off; knocked down, but still have some life in us" (II Cor 4:6–9). [...]

It is obvious, then, that the first individuals who spread Christianity were perfectly aware that the divine shone forth in the world from what they said and did, that their words were insufficient, their gestures weak, their personalities inadequate, their human condition wretched.

However, this did not mean that they were acquiescent and resigned. No, they proudly ran the race, fought the daily struggle, constantly reaching out for the gift of salvation.

Moreover, it was not merely the people through whom God communicated himself who were human in a perfectly ordinary way. The circumstances were also unexceptional. We are reminded that in the day-to-day life of the first Christian communities, man's encounter with God – the supreme aspect of the problem of life – and his participation in his being took place, above all, in situations we might call vulgar, in the most normal of suppers, a simple, shared meal. This was the context in which the deepest, most mysterious involvement with the Lord transpired, the communication of divine life with all its gifts came through eating bread and drinking wine. Certainly, man may well feel such a method to be the most banal of approaches; he may show a type of subtle resistance to God's mysterious method of wanting to pass through human reality (while man, in contrast, tends to codify all his thinking and doing as divine!).

However, this is the chosen method: God communicates himself in the human realm, even the word which pardons sin (and who can pardon sin except God?) is a human word, channelled through a pathetic human voice. "If you forgive anyone's sins, they are forgiven; if you retain anyone's sins, they are retained" (John 20: 23).

It is not so easy to realize in existential terms that this is precisely the problem of the Church: God *wants* to pass through the humanity of all those he has taken hold of in Baptism. [...]

Let us summarize: the Church is characterized by the divine which has chosen human reality to communicate himself. This implies that we accept human factors as part and parcel of the definition of Church. Given our human limitations, it seems absurd that God would choose us in this way. But if we recognize that *this* is the Church's definition of itself, then no objection to Christianity that makes a point or pretext of the disproportion, inadequacy, or error of the human reality which forms the Church, can ever logically be raised. In the same way, in reverse, a true Christian will not be able to use his limits as an excuse, even though, by definition, he will have limits. As we have seen in St Paul, a Christian, while being intent on asking for the Lord's goodness, will, at the same time, be sincere and sorrowful in judging his own incapacity, which, nevertheless, is used by God.

A MISSION OF THE CHURCH: TOWARDS EARTHLY MAN
Why the Church? (Montreal & Kingston: McGill-Queen's University Press, 2001), 154–5

The Church's task is not to magically resolve human problems, replacing the responsibility of human freedom, but rather to put men and women in the best position in order to face them. Her task is to educate man to live every circumstance – culture, love, work, and politics – illuminated by the light of faith.

In summary, we can trace the whole gamut of human problems to four large, fundamental categories. The first problem falls within the horizon of the category of culture, and here lie all problems related to man's search for *truth* and the meaning of reality. This is the category which reveals man's conception of self in the face of his own destiny, according to which he mobilizes and utilizes the elements of his own existence. The second problem is that of *love*, and here fall all of the problems man experiences in relation to his constant search for personal completeness. The third problem is related to man's need to express his personality, all his hopes of leaving his mark on the reality of time and space that is his to live, and this can generate problems under the category of *work*. And lastly is the political problem of human co-existence with its whole comprehensive and difficult spectrum. Each of these categories groups different facets of the obstacles and problems that man must face on his journey. And although conditioned by them, an individual thinks he can resolve, forget, or even repress the fundamental needs they represent.

If the Church were to proclaim that its aim was to take over the human effort of self-advancement, self-expression, and human searching, it would be acting like the kind of parents – to return to the mother image used before – who are deluded into thinking that they can resolve their children's problems by taking their place. This would be an illusion for the Church, too, because it would mean falling short of its educational task. […]

Moreover, this illusion would also diminish the essential history of the Christian phenomenon, and it would impoverish man's journey. […]

The Church's direct task, then, is not to provide man with solutions to the problems he encounters on his way.

5 The Risk of Education

"DEMONSTRATING THE RELEVANCE OF FAITH
TO ANSWER LIFE'S NEEDS"
Il rischio educativo [The Risk of Education] (Milan: Rizzoli,
2005), 15–21

The Risk of Education, *one of his best-known books, describes Fr Giussani's fundamental concern and the theme of his entire Christian proposal: education. He lists three components in the process of educating: passing on a tradition, through a present experience, to set young people free to discover that faith is useful for their lives. Fr Giussani never presumed to impose his own way of thinking, but rather aimed to teach a method of verifying the reasonableness of the faith in a world where everything says the opposite.*

The fundamental idea behind educating young people is that they will be the actors who rebuild society; therefore, the primary concern of society is to educate young people (which is the opposite of what happens today).

The dominant theme of all of our conversations is education: how to educate ourselves, what it means to educate, and how it should be done in order for it to be a *true education*, that is, one that corresponds with our humanity. It is, then, *education of the human*, of what is original in our nature, which, though expressed differently in each of us, is substantially and fundamentally the same. Behind all the diversity of cultures and customs, the human heart is *one and the same,* including my heart and your heart, and we find the same heart in those who live far away from us, whether in other countries or continents.

The first concern for a genuine education sufficient for man is *to educate the human heart as it was made by God*. To live morally means nothing more than to continue to live as God created us, to interact with things according to the original disposition He gave us in front of all of creation.

There is much we could say about education, but what matters to us in particular are the following points:

(1) To educate, we must propose the past in a way that does it justice. Without this proposal of awareness of the past, of tradition, young people grow to be imbalanced or skeptical. If they are not presented with a "working hypothesis" favoured over others, they will either face the complicated task of inventing their own or they will become skeptical, which is more likely, because it saves them the trouble of trying to live in a way that is coherent with the hypothesis they chose.

In my book *Realtà e giovinezza: La sfida* [Youth and Reality: the Challenge], I wrote, "It is tradition, consciously embraced, that offers a comprehensive way of looking at the world. It offers a hypothesis of meaning and a clear image of our destiny." Thus, one enters the world with a clear image of destiny, with a hypothesis of meaning that does not come from a book: the hypothesis *is* the heart, as we said before. The text continues, "Tradition is like a working hypothesis that man is armed with by nature so he can evaluate all things."[1]

(2) The second priority of education is that the past must be presented to young people *from within an experience lived in the present* which helps them to see how it corresponds to the ultimate needs of the human heart. I reiterate: it must be within a life that proves its own merit in the present. Only a lived experience can present, or even has the right and duty to present tradition, the past, as a hypothesis for life. However, if the past is neglected, if it is not presented within a living experience full of reasons, it will also be impossible to reach the third necessary step for education: a critical evaluation.

(3) True education must be an *education in criticism*. Until about the age of ten (though now it may end even earlier), a child still repeats, "Teacher said so; my mom said so." Why is this? Because it is natural for those who love the child to hand on to him or her, to put in their "backpack" for life, the best of what they have lived and chosen in life. At some point, however, it is natural that the child, or one who was once a child, instinctively take the backpack, put it in front of himself to evaluate it (we get the English word "problem" from the Greek *probállo*, to "put forward,"). What we were told must become a "problem" for us! If it never becomes a problem, its content will never mature in us and we will either reject or cling to it irrationally.

Once one has the backpack in front of himself, he rummages through it. Again in Greek, the word *krinein, krísis*, the origin of the word "critique," is used to express this. Criticism, therefore, means to delve into the reasons for things; it does not necessarily have a negative connotation.

The young person digs through his pack, and with this capacity for critique, he takes what he finds inside, all that has been given to him through tradition, with the desires he finds in his heart; because we find the ultimate criteria to judge within ourselves, otherwise it would feel alien to us. This ultimate criterion is shared by each of us; it is the need for truth, beauty, and goodness. Even considering all the ways that our imagination can embellish each of these needs, all actions begin from these fundamental impulses, though they may later take shape in different ways according to the individual circumstances of each person's experience.

Our insistence is upon the *education in criticism:* a child receives a patrimony from the past, communicated to him by engaging him in a present experience, which presents that past, giving reasons for what it says. Then he must take that past and its explanations and evaluate them, comparing them with what he finds in his heart and say, "it's true" or "it's not true" or "I doubt it." Through this process, with the help of companionship (without this companionship, man would be at the mercy of the tempests and fickleness of his heart, in the instinctive understanding of the word "heart"), he can say "yes" or he can say "no." In doing so, he takes on his stature as a man.

Too often, we have been afraid of this critical capacity. Others, those who were afraid of it, have wielded it without understanding it well, and have used it poorly.

Criticism has become equated with negativity, as has questioning something that someone has told you. If I tell you something, then you question it, asking yourself, "Is it true?," this has been equated with doubt or rejection of what was said. The identity of a question with definitive doubt has been disastrous for young people's identity today.

Doubts bring the search for truth to an end (which may or may not last), but a question, or a problem, is an invitation to understand what is in front of us, to discover something new that is good and true; it is an invitation to a richer and more mature sense of fulfillment.

Without these three factors: *tradition*, an *experience lived in the present* and the reasons for it, and *criticism* – I'm so thankful to my father, who always taught me to look at things and ask why; who would tell me each night before going to bed, "You always have to ask why. Ask yourself why," (though he said it for very different reasons) – young people will be like fragile leaves far from the branch that supports them, subject to the changes of the strongest wind; subject to public opinion manufactured by whoever is in power: "Where are you going?" as the Italian poet Leopardi wrote.[2]

Our goal is to free young people from the mental slavery that binds them, from the conformity in which their thoughts are enslaved by the opinions of others.

From my first day of teaching, I always said, "I'm not here so that you can take my ideas as your own; I'm here to teach you a true method that you can use to judge the things I will tell you. And what I have to tell you is the result of a long experience, of a two-thousand-year-old history."

We have been careful to respect this method throughout our efforts to educate and have tried to clearly explain the reason for the method: to demonstrate the relevance of faith to answer life's needs. Through my education at home and my time of formation in seminary, and later through my own meditation, I was thoroughly persuaded that a faith that could not be found or confirmed in present experience, that was not useful to its needs, would not be a faith capable of standing up in a world in which everything, *everything*, says the opposite. This opposition was so deep that, for a long time, even theology became a victim of the diluting of truth.

Our goal is to show the relevance of faith to answer the needs of life, and therefore – this "therefore" is very important for me – to demonstrate the reasonableness of the faith, but we must give a precise definition to understand reason. To say that faith exalts our reason is to say that faith corresponds to the fundamental and original needs of every human heart. We see the use of the word "heart" to describe what we might call "reason" in the Bible. Faith responds to the original needs of the human heart, which are the same for everyone: the need for truth, beauty, goodness, justice, love, and one's complete satisfaction, which – as I often emphasize with young people – refers to the same thing as one's "perfection." (In Latin, *satisfacere* or *satisfieri* mean the same thing as *perficere*, or perfection. Perfection and satisfaction are the same thing, as are happiness and eternity.)

So when we say something is reasonable, we mean that it corresponds to the fundamental needs of the human heart, those needs that man – whether he wants to or not, or is aware of them or not – uses to judge everything, with varying degrees of success.

Considering all we have said, to give the reasons for faith means to constantly expand upon and deepen our description of the effect that Christ's presence has on the world, through the life of the Church inasmuch as it is faithful, "guarded" by the Pope in Rome. This is the transformation of life that faith proposes.

6 Prayer

PRAYER: AWARENESS OF DEPENDENCE
Alla ricerca del volto umano [In Search of the Human Face] (Milan: Rizzoli, 1995), 141–5

In this excerpt, Fr Giussani describes prayer, "becoming aware of God," as the most human of all acts. It is to be aware of our original dependence on the Father and to cry out, begging that His Kingdom come and His will be done. The one who asks is the one who is aware of his own need, which is so deep that no human effort could satisfy it, and so he cries out to the Mystery who gives life and breath to all things.

(1) St Augustine defined prayer as *Elevatio mentis in Deum*. We could translate it as "becoming aware of God."

What does it mean to become aware of God? In the end, it is to become aware of our own original dependence. Not simply dependence in the past, that our life depended on the act that created us – as a child, born *ex voluntate carnis* (of the will of the flesh), depends on his father – but a total, continual dependence in every moment and for every action. Every moment and every act of our existence has its origin in the mystery of Being; this is our true Father, the Father who continuously generates our existence. *Tam Pater, nemo* (No one else is a father to such a degree).

Human beings are distinguished from other creatures in that they are aware of what they are living. This consciousness does not reach its fullness unless it goes so far as to understand the Foundation that is the origin of life; reflection is incomplete unless it arrives at that Point that is the source of the "I" and all its actions. The ideal man, the man who is completely himself, is one who lives every moment with this awareness: as Jesus said, "pray without ceasing."

This is, however, impossible to man, except by means of an extremely rare grace, which corresponds to an extremely rare function in the world. This awareness of one's own being is usually clouded, and man recognizes his true self – which means he sees himself in his dependence upon God – in a halting way, with great variability. For practical purposes, we could translate the ideal that Jesus gave us as, "pray more than you are able." This is the formula of consciousness in relationship with the Ideal; it is the formula for the journey of man's freedom. It is this formula that best summarizes our existence, with its undefined parameters and accommodation for changing circumstances, while at the same time unquestionably affirming the constant urgency of our duty [to pray], which no parameter or circumstance can silence.

(2) The more that a man's awareness of this dependence is deepened and assimilated, the less it remains at an

intellectual level. Man receives an irresistible call (vocation) to life and being, and so the realization that one's life in its entirety depends on God as a stream depends on the spring from which it flows naturally leads to asking, to prayer. Therefore, the definitions that St Augustine and St Thomas Aquinas gave for prayer can go together, *Petitio decentium a Deo,* asking for things that are fitting for God. But what can we understand to be "fitting," if not "being," of things becoming fully themselves, and fulfilling the design for which they were created?

Asking for our being; this is the description of prayer in our life: asking to "be" in a true way, that the potential of our "I" be actualized. "*Thy Kingdom come, thy will be done*"; in relation to my person, His Kingdom, His will is precisely the fulfillment of that thought with which he created me. Every prayer is asking for (to use another word with the same meaning) holiness: "*Thy Kingdom come.*"

(3) Even when a prayer asks for the most contingent of material goods, deep down it is asking for His Kingdom; more specifically that His Kingdom be made present in my "I," that I be what I ought to be, what He wants me to be. It is like saying "Lord, I am asking You for this because I think it will be useful for me to become myself; but, of course, I ask You to give me what is truly most helpful, and not only what seems to be so to me, because I ask for Your Kingdom, and not for things as I see them." It is the same prayer that Jesus made: "Father, if possible, let this cup pass me by; but not my will, but Thine be done."

A prayer without this caveat, whether explicit or implicit, would not be a genuine asking, but rather the attempt to impose my will. Instead of expressing the awareness of dependence, it would be rebellion. It would be an absurd presumption to be able to constrain God's measure, to make what is eternal submit itself to what is ephemeral, or to make infinite wisdom bend to the capriciousness of an infant.

(4) Like every spiritual reality in this world, prayer becomes truer in humble obedience to certain "technical" conditions regarding its form. Below we have listed a few.

(*a*) The first condition in order to fulfill our duty to pray is the first condition for any earthly personal expression: *time*. Even better, we could say *to give a part of our time* to God is already prayer. This chunk of time set aside, decidedly reserved for Him, as a symbol of our dependence on Him, can itself be a form of prayer in times when our soul seems incapable of expressing itself because of aridity, tiredness, or some other deficiency.

(*b*) Next, we have to face the question of how to fill this time set aside. We fill it using the forms of expression that are natural to man: *thought, word, and action*.

Thought by itself, in the form of mental dialogue, is a genuine prayer (*meditation*). A more specific form is fixing one's consciousness upon a divine truth, or upon the very person of God, or a symbol that points to him. This is the highest form of prayer possible (*contemplation*).

Words are the most common tools that the "I" uses to express its awareness, which happens in a very unique, personal way. Speaking with God, then, is the height of personal expression. Any concern or interest that the "I" feels can be voiced, because deep down every interest that we have is part of the history of our life that God is guiding.

Like our words, our actions always go along with the awareness of an idea or a sentiment, because man is unified. This means that translating inner awareness to a behaviour or physical action in prayer can be a sign of maturity of awareness, not of childishness or simple-mindedness.

In fact, we can think of many sentiments that are more adequately expressed through gestures or actions than through words.

(c) One obstacle to prayer is that man is weak and inconsistent. Knowing one's duty does not mean it will be carried out, because of a lack of desire or an apparent lack of capacity.

This is where we can see the value of *formulaic* worship, both with prayers *(fixed words)* and rites *(fixed actions)*.

When a man's soul is barren or tired or incapable, using a memorized prayer or participating in a rite connects him to that original religious experience that has been distilled in the prayer or the rite, and a bit of its warmth is communicated to him. Each of us has experienced the healing and revitalizing power of an "Our Father" said slowly. The Our Father is the prayer in which the religious experience of Christ Himself is distilled, and it is impossible to come close to Him without feeling some of His warmth. If even the ruins of ancient architecture fail to leave a mark on a man who sees them, just think what a beneficial influence and creative power the divine architecture of words and actions will have when discovered by a soul that is in love with God.

In addition, there are some prayers and rites that have been found to be such good expressions of certain experiences or feelings that the human spirit sees no reason to look for alternatives. Even in casual speech we find formulaic sayings, such as "good morning" or "hello" or "goodbye," that are so clear and concise that they seem to be irreplaceable.

An awareness of dependence that refuses to be transformed into asking, to take on flesh and move in time – we could not call this prayer, which is relationship with Being – would be to give in to nothingness. It would merely be an excuse to refuse to make any kind of effort.

PRAYER AND THE COMMUNITARIAN SPIRIT
Alla ricerca del volto umano [In Search of the Human Face], 147, 149–52

Christian prayer is never an isolated act of a solitary "I," but comes alive and is nurtured within the experience of community. Christ is the ideal of this experience; "His every act of prayer embraced every man and woman throughout time and space."

(1) One trait of human life that we see reflected in prayer is communitarian expression.

We might think that prayer, conceived as the sacred expression of man's most intimate thoughts, would lose something of its personal originality, purity, sincerity, or intensity any time that it is taken up in a communitarian form of prayer. This is an objection that secularism has ingrained in us, but that has also crept in as a confused and perhaps subconscious belief for many of the faithful who consider communal prayer almost exclusively as a limitation. They see it as something they must adjust to with as much good will as possible, as a mortification of their personality; a mortification that is unavoidable on earth, and that can be good for us, like other sacrifices, is primarily seen as a mortification.

This is a deep misconception. Yes, communal prayer has an aspect of mortification, but only to the same degree as any other duty in this life, or as any other ideal that is translated into time and space. Communal prayer does not limit the experience of the person; it is the greatest fulfillment of that experience. [...]

(2) Let us now apply the observations we have made thus far to the phenomenon of communal prayer. To make our reflection more concrete, let us take the example of the event of Sunday Mass, the Sunday "obligation." The experience can unfold in two very different ways:

(a) Here I am, in the church, for Sunday Mass, participating along with a hundred other people. I enter, isolated behind my usual interior walls of individualism and self-absorption, and this makes me consider any of the others, with whom I have no tie of personal interest or affection, either with indifference or as potentially hostile. I am alone amidst strangers, where the key word is "strange" (in Latin, "extraneous,"). They are external to me, and have nothing to do with me. I will either get bogged down by the behaviours and personalities of those hundred people that are different from me, or I will see them as curious distractions that catch my eye.

In this scenario, in order to try to be attentive as possible, I will spend all my effort trying to block out my surroundings, seeking to isolate myself as much as possible from the presence of others and forget that they are even there. For me, the Christian congregation in the house of God would become merely an association, and the action of grace within the congregation would be no more than an obligation or a commandment. Coming together would seem to be a constraint limiting the spontaneity of my inner spirit, an uncomfortable exercise that I can only tolerate through the patience of devotion and piety.

In short, the ideal participation in Mass would be that in which each person keeps to himself as much as possible.

(b) Let's look at an alternative scenario. I enter the same church along with a hundred others, and by natural terms I am a stranger among strangers – people I've never met and may never see again. At an instinctive level, they are extraneous to me, resulting in feelings of being lost or alone. I take a minute to recollect myself and enter into a deeper awareness, reminding myself of who they are for me. Opening wide my heart, I cry out to God, "Lord, accept all of those present here, because they are yours; they are mine, they are part of me. I call upon you with them and for them. Our Father, who art in heaven ..."

The more my Christian identity matures, the deeper, simpler, and more immediate the awareness of my fellow

Christians and the corresponding gesture of prayer, of gift, of *charity* will be. Rather than seeming constrained or negated, the breadth of my spirit will find itself stretched and expanded through this gesture. It will be as if my soul, in the Christian magnanimity endowed upon it, gathered close to me the many faithful present in the church, so that my soul is partially integrated with theirs. The assembly of the faithful amplifies the strength of my voice, my awareness, and my spirit in a way that is almost physical, it is so concrete. It builds me up and "exalts" me in the etymological sense: it lifts me heavenward. My prayer is in communion and for the community, and my experience of prayer, the gesture though which I express myself to God, is fuller than it has ever been.

This awareness is so great that, even if all of the others present were distracted or full of mistakes, I would be obligated to have an even greater dedication and awareness in order to accept them, my gesture of prayer would have an even richer expression, and my identity would be more fully realized. Rather than being a *scandal* or stumbling block in my journey of personal growth, that crowd of people builds me up. They push my spirit to build itself up to the height of its potential. If the hundred were instead a thousand, or ten thousand, so much more would my spirit be exalted. The more the number of the faithful, the greater my stature.

(3) All we have said about Sunday Mass can be applied to the daily aspects of our liturgical life, in song, in the Liturgy of the Hours, and other prayers said together.

The more this communitarian spirit is understood and embraced, the more that beauty and power is present in the act of liturgy, singing, or praying the hours. They become more *harmonious*, even in the superficial, exterior sense.

Christ is the living ideal of this communitarian dimension, because His every act of prayer embraced all men, throughout time and space, like a Giant who walked the road of human existence. It is amazing to consider how the power of the communitarian unity can overcome every objection and contradiction: Christ's gestures of prayers take up those who would kill him; forgiveness is a sign of the all-powerful freedom of communitarian charity.

If we try to imagine where this ideal attitude of Christ is best imitated, we might think of the cloister, where the charity of the conscious dedication to humanity is lived out without interruption, and where that charity is expressed in a form of prayer that is perennially communal.

The cloister, however, is not outside of the experience of any Christian. Its role in the life of a religious community is a model and reminder of the loving and Catholic "space" that should be built up in the most seemingly insignificant actions of the daily life of every Christian, wherever and in whatever situation they find themselves.

Every act of prayer renews our awareness of the Presence of Christ, who is present here and now, and is an act of obedience, meaning of conversion to be more like Him.

(1) The one problem of life is the problem of faith: "My just one shall live by faith."

The work we have to do in order to comprehend the meaning of the words in the Bible points to how the labour of life is conversion; in other words, *faith*. Faith is the recognition of the presence of an Other in our midst and accepting that Other as the meaning of myself.

This requires a change in how we conceive of ourselves, in that to affirm ourselves as the subject of our actions, we must affirm an Other; we must "obey" an Other. This change in how we conceive of ourselves is the "metanoia," or conversion, of the Gospels.

"I know nothing but Christ, and Him crucified." I know *this* Christ in history, to him *this* happened. I know nothing other than Christ, who is made known through certain actions and events, and so, despite living "in the flesh," in a dynamic of life that is experientially human, I live another dynamic, that of "faith in the Son of God." I live with this new awareness of my being.

(2) To surrender to that life which faith makes me live, to recognize this in the deep, existential sense; in other words, to live the faith despite living in the flesh, is the definition of charity. It is to live a relationship of love with Being.

7 Christ, Who Begs for Man's Heart

"IN THE SIMPLICITY OF MY HEART I HAVE GLADLY GIVEN YOU EVERYTHING"
Fr Luigi Giussani's testimony during the meeting of the Holy Father John Paul II with the ecclesiastical movements and the new communities. St Peter's Square, Rome, 30 May 1998; in L. Giussani, S. Alberto, and J. Prades, Generating Traces in the History of the World (Montreal & Kingston: McGill-Queen's University Press, 1998), ix–xii.

In this witness addressed to the whole Church, given at the audience with Pope John Paul II on 30 May 1998 in St Peter's Square, Fr Giussani summarizes his path of faith and the significance of Christ for his life. His words are a remarkable documentation of what happens in the life of a man who lets himself be overtaken by the Christian event. One becomes a presence that "makes the essential, which is Jesus Christ, visible," as Pope Francis would say in his invitation to the Church and all her baptized to take on the one task given to us who have received the message of Christ who died and is risen.

I shall try to say how an attitude was born in me – an attitude that God was to bless, as He wished – and that I could not have foreseen nor even wished for.

(1) "What is man that you should keep him in mind, mortal man that you care for him?" (Ps 8:4). No question in life has ever struck me like this one. There has been only one Man in the world who could answer me, by asking another question, "What would it profit a man if he gain the whole world, and then lose himself? Or what could a man give in exchange for himself?" (Mt 16:26; see Mk 8:36ff; Lk 9:25f). I was never asked a question that took my breath away so much as this question of Christ's! No woman ever heard another voice speak of her son with such an original tenderness and unquestionable valuing of the fruit of her womb, with such a wholly positive affirmation of its destiny; only the voice of the Jew, Jesus of Nazareth. And more than that, no man can feel his own dignity and absolute value affirmed far beyond all his achievements. No one in the world has ever been able to speak like this!

Only Christ takes my humanity so completely to heart. This is the wonder expressed by Dionysius the Areopagite (fifth century): "Who could ever speak to us of the love that Christ has for man, overflowing with peace?" (Dionysius the Areopagite, *De divinis Nominibus* 953 A 10). I've been repeating these words to myself for more than fifty years!

This is why *Redemptor Hominis* appeared on our horizon like a beam of light in the thick darkness covering the earth of present-day man, with all his confused questions.

Thank you, Your Holiness.

It was a simplicity of heart that made me feel and recognize Christ as exceptional, with that certain promptness that marks the unassailable and indestructible evidence of factors and moments of reality, which, on entering the horizon of our person, pierce us to the heart.

So the acknowledgment of who Christ is in our lives invades the whole of our awareness of living: "I am the Way, the Truth and the Life" (John 14:6). "*Domine Deus, in simplicitate cordis mei laetus obtuli universa*" (Lord God, in the simplicity of my heart I have gladly given You everything), says the Offertory Prayer of the ancient Ambrosian Liturgy.[1] What shows that this acknowledgment is true is the fact that life has an ultimate, tenacious capacity for gladness.

(2) How can this gladness, which is the human glory of Christ, and which fills my heart and my voice in some moments, be found to be true and reasonable to today's man? Because that Man, the Jew, Jesus of Nazareth, died for us and rose again. That Risen Man is the Reality on which all the positivity of every man's existence depends.

Every earthly experience lived in the Spirit of Jesus, Risen from the dead, blossoms in Eternity. This blossoming will not bloom only at the end of time; it has already begun on the dawn of Easter. Easter is the beginning of this journey to the eternal Truth of everything, a journey that is therefore already within man's history. For Christ, as the Word of God made flesh, makes Himself present as the Risen one in every period of time, throughout the whole of history, in order to reach from Easter morning to the end of this time, the end of this world. The Spirit of Jesus, that is to say of the Word made flesh, becomes an experience possible for ordinary man, in His power to redeem the whole existence of each person and human history, in the radical change that He produces in the one who encounters Him, and, like John and Andrew, follows Him.

Thus for me the grace of Jesus, in so far as I have been able to adhere to the encounter with Him and communicate Him to the brothers in God's Church, has become the experience of a faith that in the Holy Church, that is to say the Christian People, revealed itself as a call and a desire to feed a new Israel of God: "*Populum Tuum vidi, cum ingenti gaudio, Tibi offerre donaria*" ("With great joy, I saw your People, acknowledging existence as an offering to You"), continues the liturgical prayer.

So it was that I saw a people taking shape, in the name of Christ. Everything in me became truly more religious, with my awareness striving to discover that "God is all in all" (I Cor 15:28).

In this people gladness was becoming "*ingenti gaudio,*" that is to say the decisive factor of one's own history as ultimate positivity and therefore as joy.

What could have seemed at most to be an individual experience was becoming a protagonist in history, and so an instrument of the mission of the one People of God. This now is the foundation of the search for an expressed unity among us.

(3) That precious text of the Ambrosian Liturgy concludes with these words: "*Domine Deus, custodi hanc vol-*

untatem cordis eorum" ("Lord God, keep safe this attitude of their heart").

Infidelity always arises in our hearts even before the most beautiful and true things; the infidelity in which, before God's humanity and man's original simplicity, man can fall short, out of weakness and worldly preconception, like Judas and Peter. Even this personal experience of infidelity that always happens, revealing the imperfection of every human action, makes the memory of Christ more urgent.

The desperate cry of Pastor Brand in Ibsen's play of the same name ("Answer me, O God, in the hour in which death is swallowing me up: is the whole of man's will not enough to achieve even a part of salvation?"),[2] is answered by the humble positivity of St Theresa of the Child Jesus who writes, "When I am charitable it is only Jesus who is acting in me."[3] All this means that man's freedom, which the Mystery always involves, has *prayer* as its supreme, unassailable expressive form. This is why freedom, according to the whole of its true nature, posits itself as an entreaty to adhere to Being, therefore to Christ. Even in man's incapacity, in man's great weakness, affection for Christ is destined to last.

In this sense Christ, Light and Strength for every one of his followers, is the adequate reflection of that word with which the Mystery appears in its ultimate relationship with the creature, as *mercy*: *Dives in Misericordia*. The mystery of mercy shatters any image of complacency or despair; even the feeling of forgiveness lies within this mystery of Christ.

This is the ultimate embrace of the Mystery, against which man – even the most distant, the most perverse or the most obscured, the most in the dark – cannot oppose anything, can make no objection. He can abandon it, but in so doing he abandons himself and his own good. The Mystery as mercy remains the last word even on all the awful possibilities of history.

For this reason existence expresses itself, as ultimate ideal, in *begging*. The real protagonist of history is the beggar: Christ who begs for man's heart, and man's heart that begs for Christ.

8 "Woman, Do Not Weep!"

"THE GLORY OF GOD IS MAN WHO LIVES"
Msgr Luigi Giussani's closing talk at the Retreat of the Fraternity of Communion and Liberation, Rimini, 5 May 2002

Fr Giussani takes us back two thousand years, making us spectators to the facts and events of the Gospels. Through this immediacy, his greeting to the tens of thousands of attendees at the end of a weekend of Spiritual Exercises brought to life the encounter of Jesus with the widow of Nain, "Man, woman, boy, girl; you, all of you: Don't cry! Don't cry! There is a gaze and a heart that penetrates and understands all of you, down to the marrow of your bones."

That evening, Jesus was interrupted, stopped on his journey to the village towards which He was heading, to which He had headed out, because loud weeping was heard from a woman, with a cry of pain that shook the hearts of all those present, but that shook, has shaken Christ's heart first of all (see Luke 7:11–16).

"Woman, do not weep!" (Luke 7:13) He had never seen her, never met her before.

"Woman, do not weep!" What support could she have, that woman as she listened to the words that Jesus said to her?

"Woman, do not weep!" When we return home, when we go on the bus, when we climb aboard the train, when we see the cars lined up in the streets, when we think about all the jumble of things that are involved in the lives of millions and millions of people, hundreds of millions of people. How decisive is the look that a child or a "great" adult would have turned on this Man who was coming along at the head of a small group of friends and had never seen that woman, but halted when the sound, the reverberation of her weeping reached Him! "Woman, do not weep!" – as though no one knew her, no one could recognize her more intensely, more totally, more decisively than He!

"Woman, do not weep!" When we see – as I said to you before – all the movement in the world, in whose river, in whose streams all men present themselves to life and make life present to them, the unknown of the end is nothing but the unknown of how this newness has been reached, this newness that makes us come upon a Man, makes us encounter a Man never seen before who, faced with the pain of this woman He sees for the first time, says to her, "Woman, do not weep! Woman, do not weep!"

"Woman, do not weep!" This is the heart with which we are placed before the gaze and the sadness, before the pain of all the people with whom we come into contact, in the street, along our way, in our travels.

"Woman, do not weep!" What an unimaginable thing it is that God – "God," He who is making the whole world at this moment – seeing and listening to man, could say, "Man, do not weep!" "You, do not weep!" "Do not weep, because I did not make you for death, but for life! I put you in the world and placed you in a great company of people!"

Man, woman, boy, girl, you, all of you, do not weep! Do not weep! There is a gaze and a heart that penetrates to your very marrow and loves you all the way to your destiny, a gaze and a heart that no one can deflect from His course, no one can render incapable of saying what He thinks and what He feels, no one can render powerless!

"Gloria Dei vivens homo." (The glory of God is man who lives.)[1] The glory of God, the greatness of Him who makes the stars in the sky, who puts into the sea, drop by drop, all the blue that defines it, is man who lives.

There is nothing that can suspend that immediate rush of love, of attachment, of esteem, of hope, because He became hope for each one who saw Him, who heard Him: "Woman, do not weep!," who heard Jesus say this: "Woman, do not weep!"

There is nothing that can block the certainty of a destiny that is mysterious and good!

We are together, saying to each other, "You – I have never seen you, I don't know who you are: Do not weep!" Because weeping is your destiny, it seems to be your unavoidable destiny: "Man, do not weep!"

"Gloria Dei vivens homo." The glory of God – the glory for whom He holds up the world, the universe – is man who lives, every man who lives: the man who lives, the woman who weeps, the woman who smiles, the child, the woman who dies a mother.

"Gloria Dei vivens homo." We want this and nothing but this, that the glory of God be manifested to all the world and touch all the spheres of earth: the leaves, all the leaves of the flowers and all the hearts of men.

We have never seen each other, but this is what we see among us, what we feel among us.

Ciao!

9 "Simon, Do You Love Me?"

"BIRTH OF NEW MORALITY"
Generating Traces in the History of the World, with
S. Alberto and J. Prades (Montreal & Kingston: McGill-
Queen's University Press, 2010), 59–63

In this excerpt, Fr Giussani describes the episode of Peter and Jesus on the shore of Lake Tiberias, as he did thousands of times in his life. Giussani considers the three-fold "yes" of Peter to Jesus's question, "Simon, do you love me?," repeated three times, the beginning of a new morality that is not the result of human effort, but is a gift that Jesus gives to those who surrender to the attraction of His presence. Only He has the power to transform life, because He has won the victory over sin and death.

"Simon, Do You Love Me?"

The twenty-first chapter of John's Gospel is a fascinating documentation of the historical birth of the new ethic. The particular story narrated there is the keystone of the Christian conception of man, of his morality, in his relationship with God, with life and with the world.

The disciples were on their way back, at dawn, after a terrible night's fishing on the lake, in which they had caught nothing. As they approach the shore, they see a figure on the beach preparing a fire. Later they would notice that there were some fish on the fire collected for them, for their early-morning hunger. All of a sudden, John says to Peter, "That's the Lord!" They all open their eyes and Peter throws himself into the water, just as he is, and reaches the shore first. The others follow suit. They sit down in a circle in silence; no one speaks, because they all know it is the Lord. Sitting down to eat, they exchange a few words, but they are all fearful at the exceptional presence of Jesus, the Risen Jesus, who had already appeared to them at other times.

Simon, whose many errors had made him humbler than all the others, sat down, too, before the food prepared by the Master. He looks to see who is next to him and is terrified to see that it is Jesus himself. He turns his gaze away from Him and sits there all embarrassed. But Jesus speaks to him. Peter thinks in his heart, "My God, My God, what a dressing-down I deserve! Now he is going to ask me, 'Why did you betray me?'" The betrayal had been the last great error he had made, but, in spite of his familiarity with the Master, his whole life had been a stormy one, because of his impetuous character, his instinctive stubbornness, his tendency to act on impulse. He now saw himself in the light of all his defects. That betrayal had made him more aware of all his other errors, of the fact that he was worthless, weak, miserably weak. "Simon…" – who knows how he must have trembled as that word sounded in his ears and touched his heart? – "Simon…" – here he would have begun to turn his face towards Jesus – "Do you love me?" Who on earth would have expected that question? Who would have expected those words?"

Peter was a forty- or fifty-year-old man, with a wife and children, and yet he was such a child before the mystery of that companion he had met by chance! Imagine how he felt transfixed by that look that knew him through and through. "You will be called *Kefas* (cf. 1 John: 42)." His tough character was described by that word "rock," and the last thing he had in mind was to imagine what the mystery of God and the mystery of that Man – the Son of God – had to do with that rock, to that rock. From the first encounter, He filled his whole mind, his whole heart. With that presence in his heart, with the continuous memory of Him, he looked at his wife and children, his work-mates, friends and strangers, individuals and crowds, he thought, and fell asleep. That Man had become for him like an immense revelation, still to be clarified.

"Simon, do you love me?" "Yes, Lord, I love you." How could he say such a thing after all he had done? That *yes* was an affirmation acknowledging a supreme excellence, an undeniable excellence, a sympathy that overwhelmed all others. Everything remained inscribed in that look. Coherence or incoherence seemed to fall into second place behind the faithfulness that felt like flesh of his flesh, behind the form of life which that encounter had moulded.

In fact, no reproof came, only the echo of the same question: "Simon, do you love me?" Not uncertain, but fearful and trembling, he replied again, "Yes, I love You." But the third time, the third time that Jesus threw the question at him, he had to ask confirmation from Jesus himself: "Yes, Lord, You know I love You. All my human preference is for You, all the preference of my mind, all the preference of my heart; You are the extreme preference of life, the supreme excellence of things. I don't know, I don't know how, I don't know how to say it and I don't know how it can be but, in spite of all I have done, in spite of all I can still do, I love You."

This *yes* is the birth of morality, the first breath of morality in the dry desert of instinct and pure reaction. Morality sinks its roots into this Simon's *yes*, and this *yes* can take root in man's soil only thanks to a dominant Presence, understood, accepted, embraced, served with all the energy of your heart; only in this way can man become a child again. Without a Presence, there is no moral act, there is no morality.

But why is Simon's *yes* to Jesus the birth of morality? Don't the criteria of coherence and incoherence come first?

Peter had done just about all the wrong he could do, yet he lived a supreme sympathy for Christ. He understood that everything in him tended to Christ, that everything was gathered in those eyes, in that face, in that heart. His past sins could not amount to an objection, nor even the incoherence he could imagine for the future. Christ was the source, the place of his hope. Had someone objected to what he had done or what he might have done, Christ remained, through the gloom of those objections, the source of light for his hope. And he esteemed Him above everything else, from the first moment in which he had felt himself stared at by His eyes, looked on by Him.

This is why he loved Him.

"Yes, Lord, you know You are the object of my supreme sympathy, of my highest esteem."

This is how morality is born. The expression is very generic: "Yes, I love You." But it is as generic as it is generative of a new life to be lived.

"Whoever has this hope in him purifies himself as He is pure" (1 John 3:3). Our hope is in Christ, in that Presence that, however distracted and forgetful we be, we can no longer (not completely anyway) remove from the earth of our heart because of the tradition through which He has reached us. It is in Him that I hope, before counting my errors and my virtues. Numbers have nothing to do with this. In the relationship with Him, numbers don't count, the weight that is measured or measurable is irrelevant, and all the evil I can possibly do in the future has no relevance either. It cannot usurp the first place that this *yes* of Simon, repeated by me, has before the eyes of Christ. So a kind of flood comes from the depths of our heart, like a breath that rises from the breast and pervades the whole person, making it act, making it want to act more justly. The flower of the desire for justice, for true, genuine love, the desire to be capable of acting gratuitously, springs up from the depths of the heart. Just as our every move starts off not from an analysis of what the eyes see, but from an embrace of what the heart is waiting for, in the same way perfection is not the keeping of rules, but adhesion to a Presence.

Only the man who lives this hope in Christ lives the whole of his life in ascesis, in striving for good. And even when he is clearly contradictory, he desires the good. This always conquers, in the sense that it is the last word on himself, on his day, on what he does, on what he has done, on what he will do in the future. The man who lives this hope in Christ keeps on living in ascesis. Morality is a continual striving towards "perfection" that is born of an event that is a *sign* of a relationship with the divine, with the Mystery.

The Ultimate Reason for the Yes

What is the true reason for the *yes* that Simon answers to Christ? Why does the *yes* said to Christ matter more than listing all your errors and the possible future errors that your weakness forebodes? Why is this *yes* more decisive and greater than all the moral responsibility expressed in its details, in concrete practice? The answer to this question reveals the ultimate essence of the One sent by the Father. Christ is the One "sent" by the Father; He is the One who reveals the Father to men and to the world. "This is true life: that they may know You, the only true God, and the one You have sent, Jesus Christ" (John 17:3). The most important thing is that "they know You," that they love You, because this You is the meaning of life.

"Yes, I love You," Peter said. And the reason for this *yes* consisted in the fact that in those eyes that had set on him that first time, and had set on him so many other times during the following days and years, he had glimpsed who God was, who Yahweh was, the true Yahweh: *mercy*.[1] God's relationship with his creature is revealed in Jesus as love, and therefore as mercy. Mercy is the attitude of the Mystery towards any kind of weakness, error and forgetfulness on man's part: in the face of any crime that man commits, God loves him.

Simon felt this. This is where his "Yes, I love You" comes from.

The meaning of the world and of history is the mercy of Christ, Son of the Father, sent by the Father to die for us. In Milosz's play *Miguel Mañara* Miguel was going to the Abbot every day to weep over his past sins. One day the Abbot tells him, somewhat impatiently, "Stop weeping like a woman. All this never existed." What does he mean by "never existed"? Miguel had murdered, raped, he had done all kinds of things ... "All this never existed. Only He is."[2] He, Jesus, addresses us, becomes an "encounter" for us, asking us only one thing; not "What have you done?" but "Do you love me?"

10 Charity: The Gift of the Self, Moved

"GOD WAS MOVED BY OUR NOTHINGNESS"
Is It Possible to Live This Way?, vol. 3, *Charity* (Montreal
& Kingston: McGill-Queen's University Press, 2009), 7–18

*Charity is first and foremost not a human initiative, but an act
of God. Deus caritas est – God is love, as Pope Benedict XVI
says in his first encyclical. Accordingly, Fr Giussani speaks of
charity as "a total gift of Self," the supreme act of the Creator's
uncalculating generosity towards creation. Why should Christ
"die for me? What explains the most extreme gift of self that
we could imagine?" Human charity, therefore, is a gift of self,
being moved; it is the imitation of Christ who was moved by our
nothingness.*

Two things make up the Christian characteristic of charity. Charity is a word everyone can use: "Do it for me
out of charity, Mr. Deputy: give me this post on the ad-
visory board. Do it out of charity!" We instead, will
speak today of the authentic and Christian concept of
charity, that is, of the true concept of love. Why is charity the true concept of love? Because the reason for it is

the exhaustive reason, the only one, the exhaustive one, of love: the reason of love that identifies the object it desires with the other's good, the other's destiny. How can we succeed in understanding the figure of Christ or read a page of the gospel with intelligence and the necessary emotion if we don't keep this in mind? Why did Jesus look around Him? Excuse me, why is Carlo interested in you? I remember that day when he came to tell me that his professor would give him the Chair of Chemistry at the University of Palermo. And he said: "I am going to refuse it, because if I accept it, I will lose my vocation." What was his vocation if not that which you see him doing? For whom? For you. And who are you? Who makes him do it?

(a) *A pure gift of self.* First of all, God's relationship with man, the Mystery's relationship with man – let's say the Mystery, because Mystery is God and Christ, it is God and man – the Mystery appears to man as gratuitousness, that is, as charity. You can even say what St John said: God's very nature is charity (I John 4:16). Nature is that factor by which one acts in a certain way; nature is the origin of actions, therefore, if one acts with charity, it is because he has the nature that is the origin of charity. And in fact he says: "*Deus charitas est*," God is love, but love in its total, absolute sense: it wants the other's good.

God's nature appears as gratuitousness insomuch as He gives Himself to man. Gift: this is the first word the term "gratuitousness," or the term "charity" or the term "love" attaches itself to. It is a pure gift, we said: without something in return. Expecting nothing in return means that it is a pure gift. God's nature is to give, He appears to man as giving, as a gift, without expecting something in return – a pure gift.

What does He give you? Himself, which is to say, Being – Being, because without Him nothing of what was made was made. "Without me you can do nothing" (John 15:5): imagine that scene, the night of Holy Thursday. Everything was against them, and Jesus spoke, spoke – that long discourse we read together on Holy Thursday.[1] Those men who were accustomed to hearing Him speak stared at Him while He spoke, observing all His actions; they were more attentive to Him than usual; everyone was attentive. That man who had put His hand in the dish to eat together with them – as they did back then – at a certain point interrupts and says: "Without me you can do nothing." This is God, the only one who can say this is God!

God's nature appears to man as an absolute gift: God gives Himself, gives His very self to man. And what is God? The source of being. God gives man being: He gives man the ability to be; He gives man the ability to be greater, to grow; He gives man the ability to be completely himself, to grow to fulfillment; that is, He gives man the ability to be happy (happy – that is, totally satisfied or perfect. As I've always said, in Latin and in Greek, "perfect" and "satisfied" are the same word: *perfectus*, that is, perfect or fulfilled. A man who is fulfilled is a man who is satisfied).

He gave Himself to me by giving me His being: "Let us make man in our own image and likeness" (Genesis 1:26). And then, when man least expected it – he couldn't even dream about it, he no longer expected it, he no longer thought about Him from whom he had received being – this "Him" re-enters man's life to save it. He gives Himself again, dying for man. He gives everything, a total gift of self, until: "There is no greater love than to lay down one's life for one's friends" (John 15:13). A total gift.

But here, there is a final nuance. What Christ gives us in dying for us – dying because we betrayed Him – so as to purify us from the betrayal, is greater than what was owed to us. This is like an angle opened to the infinite, to be considered as you go through your life, something to be experienced. Christ gives us more than what was necessary to save us: where sin abounds, gratuitousness overabounds. He did more than what was necessary to save us. To save us, Christ could have merely said: "Father, forgive them"; that was enough. While He reclined to eat the last supper, he could have said: "Father, forgive them." That would have been enough. It would even have been enough for him to say: "Yes, Father, send me," and enter into Mary's womb, becoming a baby, becoming a man. This alone would have been enough. But no: "Where sin abounded, grace overflowed all the more" (Romans 5:20). However, the fundamental concept that explains the entire value of the term charity or gratuitousness – which delineates God's nature, God's way of acting, which we must imitate because He is the Father – is the gift of self. Morality is the gift of self, like the eighth chapter in the second book of the School of Community explains.[2] Not only that, but it forgives man's betrayal, man's disregard, his denial ...

To understand what betrayal is, my friends, we have to think of our own distraction, because it is a betrayal to spend days, weeks, months ... what about last night, when did we think of Him? When did we seriously think of Him, with our heart, in this last month, in the last three months, from October until now? Never. We haven't thought of Him like John and Andrew thought of Him while they watched Him speak. If we asked a lot of questions about Him, it was out of curiosity, analysis, the need for analysis, for research, for clarification, for clarification. But we need to think the way one who is really in love thinks about his beloved (even in this case it happens extremely rarely because everything is calculated to get something in return!); solely in a way that is absolutely, totally detached – a sole desire for the good... so much so that if the other doesn't respond in kind, the desire for the other's good is nourished even more!

(b) *Moved*. The second factor – the first is the essential one – is like an adjective next to a noun, it's descriptive. Adjective means that it rests, it rests on the noun, therefore it would be secondary with respect to the first. Nevertheless, it is the most impressive, and we – I am willing to bet you – have never thought of it and would never think of it, if God had not put us together.

Why does God dedicate Himself to me? Why does He give Himself to me, in creating me, giving me being, that is, Himself (He gives me Himself, that is, being)? Moreover, why does He become man and give Himself to me to make me innocent once again – as today's hymn says[3] – and die for me (which there was absolutely no need for: a snap of the fingers and the Father would have certainly done it)? Why does He die for me? Why this gift of self up to the conceivable extreme, beyond the conceivable extreme?

Here you must go and see and learn the sentence of the prophet Jeremiah by heart, in the thirty-first chapter, from verse 3 onward. Through the voice of the prophet that is fulfilled in Christ (think of the people who were there together with that man, that young man who fulfilled these things), God says: "With eternal love I have loved you, for this I have attracted you to me [that is, I let you share in my nature], having pity on your nothingness." I have always translated this sentence in this way. What does "having pity on your nothingness" mean? What is it about? A feeling, a feeling! It is about a value that is a feeling, because affection is a feeling. To have "affection for" is a feeling, yet it is a value. To the degree that it has reason, it is a value; if it does not have reason, no type of affection is a value because it is missing half of the I, the I is truncated: only what is below the navel remains.

It is beautiful to come across this mercy − "having mercy on your nothingness" − in the gospel. For example, when − it is said twice − Jesus sees his city from the hill one night and cries over it, thinking of its ruin (Luke 13:34−5). Weeks later that city would kill Him, but for Him this doesn't matter.

Or that other night, immediately before He was taken, in the golden splendour of the temple illuminated by the setting sun, *edakruse*, the Greek text says, "He sobbed," in front of his city's destiny (Luke 19:41–4). It is pity like that of a mother who clings to her child so he doesn't fall into the mortal danger he's headed for.

And then, I'll choose from St Luke first, because in St Luke this is more noticeable than in any other gospel (St Luke with St John and St Mark with St Matthew; St Matthew was a Jew, St Luke instead was a pagan): He's walking through the countryside with his disciples and they're breaking off ears of wheat, because they were hungry. They see a funeral passing by in the nearby town. He asks: "What is it?" "It's a young guy – *adulescens*, an adolescent – who died and his mother is a widow. She lost her only son and she is a widow." In fact, the mother is wailing behind the coffin. Jesus walks over and says: "Woman, don't cry," which was something inconceivable. Aside from the fact that it's between the ridiculous and the absurd, how do you tell a woman in that condition, who follows her son's coffin "Don't cry"? It was the overflowing of pity, of compassion (Luke 7:11–17).

Or we can imagine when He passes under that tree in which Zaccheus is crouching above him: Zaccheus, the Mafia boss of the entire northeastern part of Jerusalem, of Jericho. He stops. The last thought Zaccheus had was this. He stops and looks at him: "Zaccheus [he says his name], Zaccheus, come down quickly, for today I'm going to your house" (Luke 19:1–10). There isn't any possibility of this kind of tenderness among us; we are gruesome, boorish, we are stones compared to this situation here: "Zaccheus."

Or (and these are the more symptomatic cases) when He learned that his friend Lazarus was dead: "And He wept." He was three days away – a long trip to make. As soon as He heard, He wept. So much so that the Jews who were there near him said afterward: "Could not the one who opened the eyes of the man born blind have done something about the death of His friend?" (John 11:1–44). Think of what bonds of affection there must have been.

What I want to say is that that God's charity for man – this gift of self – is made up of an emotion, of being moved. You can have compassion for a stricken animal that's dying, you can't be moved by it. For man, you can.

God's charity for man is being moved, a gift of self that vibrates, agitates, moves, is fulfilled in emotion, in the reality of being moved: it is moved. God who is moved! "What is man that you should be mindful of him?" says the psalm (Ps 8:4).

[...]

Note then the point: God was moved by our nothingness. Not only that. God was moved by our betrayal, by our crude, forgetful, and treacherous poverty, by our pettiness. God was moved by our pettiness, which is even more than being moved by our nothingness. "I have had pity on your nothingness, I have had pity on your hatred of me. I was moved because you hate me," like a father and mother who cry with emotion because of their child's hatred. They don't cry because they're struck, they cry because they are moved, which means a cry that is totally determined by the desire for the child's good, the child's destiny: that the child may change, for his destiny, for the child to be saved. It's compassion, pity, passion.

He had pity on me, the one who was so forgetful and petty. If our life is normal, with what we've had, it is difficult to be able to find particular sins during the day, but *the* sin is the pettiness of distraction and forgetfulness. The sin is the pettiness of not translating what we do into something new, not making it shine like the new dawn. Instead, we leave it opaque, we leave it as it is, without striking anyone, yet without giving it over to the splendour of Being.

He had pity on me and on my nothingness and He chose me. He chose me because He had pity on me. He chose me because He was moved by my pettiness!

What marks the devotion with which the Mystery – the supreme Mystery and the Mystery of this man who is Christ, God made man – what marks the Mystery's devotion to us, the devotion with which the Mystery creates the world and forgives man's pettiness, and forgives him while embracing him who is petty, disgusting, is an emotion, it is like an emotion; it is being moved, it has being moved within it. […]

Being Moved out of a Judgment

We must pay attention to a particular point: this being moved and this emotion bear, bring with them, a judgment and a beat of the heart. It is a judgment, therefore a value, a rational value, let's say; not inasmuch as it can be boiled down and reduced to a level that only our reason is capable of, but rational in the sense that it gives a reason, it carries its reason within it. And it becomes a *beat of the heart* for this reason. If emotion or being moved doesn't carry this judgment and this beat of the heart within them, then it is not charity. What is the reason? "I have loved you with an eternal love, therefore I have made you part of me, having pity on your nothingness." The beat of the heart is pity on your nothingness – but the reason is that you might participate in being.

11   Christ, God's Companionship with Man

THE SAME EXPERIENCE OF JOHN AND ANDREW
Easter flyer, 1982, in *Uomini senza patria* [Men Without a Homeland], *1982–83* (Milan: BUR, 2008), 8–12

Fr Giussani helps us to relive the episode of John and Andrew, who were the first of the Apostles to meet Jesus along the banks of the Jordan River. They followed him, out of curiosity and an inarticulate desire, until they came to recognize Him; "We have found the Messiah." That first encounter was the advent of new life that, in the course of history, has reached us today through the Church. In the Church, the experience of Christ – God who accompanies man – is renewed in every century, prolonging the presence of the one person in human history to say of Himself, "I am the way, the truth and the life."

Christ is the man who said He was God.

One day Philip, expressing the unspoken questions of the apostles who, in spite of having followed Jesus for some years, did not understand well (as we don't understand when we hear the word "God" or the word "Mystery"), asked Jesus: "Let us see the Father." Jesus answer-ed: "Whoever sees me sees the Father."

Christ is the only man in history who identified Himself with God, the only one who dared to say: "I am the Way, the Truth, and the Life." We, distracted by the daily routine and our superficial way of living, do not realize the boundless disproportion, the infinite distance that separated man from God. But a deeply religious soul, a religious genius realizes how great this disproportion is, and teaches it to everybody: only God is God.

This is what all the great figures in the history of religions have done, Buddha and Mohammed too. Moses was so conscious of his own smallness before God, that he pleaded with God to entrust the mission to someone else.

But amongst all these, there is one who stands out alone: this man who is Christ says He is God.

How beautiful it is, going through the Gospel, to discover that the first ones, men like us, who followed Jesus, reached the point of not realizing that this man was God, but of saying, repeating what he claimed about Himself. This is their profession of faith.

This was because the apostles did not discover that Jesus was God, but being with Him they got a big impression, so great that they "had to" say: if we are not to believe in this man, we are not to believe even our own eyes. It is because of this evidence that, even without understanding well, they repeated His words, which were to shape history and our hearts.

In the first chapter of St John's gospel, we see Jesus entering the world and history like any other man, going to listen to John the Baptist, mixed in the crowd. A moment of prophetic enlightenment forces John the Baptist to cry after Him as he walks away: "There is the Lamb of God, there is the one who takes away the sin of the world." Perhaps the people present did not pay attention to these words, as they were used to hearing strange phrases from the prophet. But there were two men there very attentive to the Baptist's every word. This unusual phrase moved them to follow Jesus: "Master where do you live?" And He: "Come and see." They went and stayed with Him the whole day. The one who is writing is one of these two, John: he remembers even the hour of the encounter, because, as he later understood, it was the hour that changed his life.

What these two announced to their friends is the offer of certainty: "We have found the Messiah." Then the friends go and see Him, talk with Him, and stay with Him for a while. Peter, Andrew, Philip, Nathaniel ... Like what happened to us: encounters that were simple, but that upset our lives. It all begins like this, through an acquaintance, the blossoming of friendship, a communion of life which goes deeper: and the more they stayed together, the more they perceived in him a power and an intelligence that leaves them breathless, an extraordinary and hitherto unknown goodness, a mastery of himself and over his own life, (he threw out a challenge to his enemies: which of you can accuse me of a contradiction, one single mistake?), a power over nature as if it were the work of his hands, an ability to conquer death: "Woman don't cry" he says to the woman of Nain, and then He raises her son to life.

Most of all, though, there is his other power: "Take heart, my son," He says to the paralytic, "your sins are forgiven." The Pharisees jump up: "What man can forgive sins: only God can do that." And Jesus replied, "Which is easier, to tell him your sins are forgiven, or tell him get up and walk? So that you know that I have the power to forgive sins, I tell you: get up and walk."

The small group of friends, men and women who followed Him and witnessed daily such great things, cannot suppress the question: "Who is He?" They know where He comes from, they know His mother and relatives, they know everything about Him, but the power of this man is so much out of proportion, He is so great and so different a personality, that every question takes a different meaning: "Who can He be?"

In exasperation even His enemies will ask the same question, "How long will you keep us with bated breath? Tell us where you come from and who you are." They had all His detail recorded, but these couldn't give them a full answer. It is Jesus Himself who gives the answer to Caiaphas who questioned Him, "I adjure you by the living God to tell us if you are the Christ the son of God?". Then Christ can no longer keep quiet, because this is the testimony that He has come to give. His "yes" to the question of Caiaphas puts the Sanhedrin in turmoil: he has blasphemed! He has called Himself God. But He had already said it "Before Abraham was, I am."

Again, when he passes with his disciples under the rock of Caesarea Philippi he asks them "Who do people say I am?"

And you, who do you say "I am?" The power of Peter's answer reaches out to us. It is not his word, he repeats the phrase that he himself has heard, "You are Christ, the Son of the living God." And Jesus' reply to Peter gets us all involved: "You are lucky, Peter, because you did not speak these words on your own accord, but my Father inspired you. Now I tell you that you are like this rock and like on this rock is built the impregnable fortress, so on you I will build my church, and nobody will ever manage to destroy it."

The question that Christ asks the apostles is the question of our life. No other question that man can think of is more grave or more decisive: the whole value of our life depends on the reply to this question; whether He existed as any other man, or exists as the man-God.

If we consider the difference between the answer of his friends and that of the crowd that refuses Him, we note that the apostles and the women were those who followed and lived with Him.

This is the highway to evidence and reason: it is the road of life, of continuous relationship, of daily sharing. This is why they could say: if we do not believe in this man we cannot even trust our own eyes. The crowd instead followed Jesus when He aroused their curiosity or when they had something to gain by it. But they were struck because His words were true. And the evidence of the truth cannot be denied. But their interest soon died: the crowd followed Him because they enjoyed hearing

Him, without committing themselves or involving their lives.

In chapter 6 of St John, Jesus, moved because people follow him, has the most fascinating intuition of His life: "You follow me because I satisfied your hunger with bread; but I will give you my flesh to eat and my blood to drink." The great disproportion of the Godhead reveals itself here, becomes evident, and it is here that begins the resistance of those who do not want to understand, of those who are scandalized because the criteria and the ways of this man upset their way of thinking.

"He is mad: who can give his flesh to eat and his blood to drink?" Angry whispering created general noise, and the whole crowd shouts and they leave the synagogue. Christ remains alone with His people in the silence of the evening. And He breaks the silence with another question: "Do you want to go away too?" "Master" – cries Peter again suddenly and impetuously – "We don't understand what you are saying either, but if we go away from you, where do we go? Only You have the word which gives meaning to our life." This is the answer of someone who has the humility, the faithfulness, and the humanity needed to follow Jesus, because he is attracted by the evidence of the truth of His words.

But whoever cannot follow, who does not dare to make the effort of becoming familiar, with the daily sharing of his life, will never manage to make the truth evident, and will not find an answer that is true, personal and mature to the fundamental, definitive question that Jesus puts them "and you, who do you say I am?"

How can we answer this question, we, who were not present at the wedding at Cana, and who did not witness the cure of the paralytic, who did not attend the funeral of Nain, who hadn't followed Him for three days in the bush, forgetting even the hunger? How can we live out the familiarity with Him, that familiarity in which His word becomes evident and the only one that gives meaning to life?

There is a way: the companionship born of Christ has erupted in history: it is the Church, His body, the mode of His presence today, a day-by-day familiarity, a commitment in the mystery of his presence within the sign that is the Church. This is how a rational evidence, fully reasonable, can be born, which makes us repeat with certainty what He, unique in the history of humanity, said of himself: I am the way, the truth, and the life.

12   How We Become Christians

"SOMETHING *OUT* OF THIS WORLD, *IN* THIS WORLD"
Notes from a talk by Luigi Giussani in the Basilica of St
Anthony, Padua, Italy, 11 February 1994, in *Come si di-
venta cristiani* [How We Become Christians] (Genoa and
Milan: Marietti 1820, 2007), 9–23

*This text describes how Christianity happens: through an en-
counter. This was true for the first Christians, just as it is for
each of us today. Spanning two thousand years of history, the
proclamation of God made man is "the best, most human, most
hopeful and promising message that a man could hear" today.*

I thank the community of the friars very much for this
invitation to come here and immerse ourselves in that
wave of grace that flowed from the words of St Anthony, as a specialist in the study of the Saint's life said
to me just now. This brought to my mind a phrase
from the early Christian writings, a phrase well
known to us: "Seek every day the faces of the saints so
that you find rest in their words."[1] So I pray St An-

thony to lighten up our faces, making them childlike, simple, poor in spirit, as the holy Gospel says – as he has lit up the faces of millions of people who came to this house of his – and that our hearts, that is, our faith, may find rest in the words we shall say, so that we not waste time and because in these sad times, when everything tends to be confused and everything seems to be fading, becoming vague, and there seem to be no more certainties, what we need above all is comfort, in its true sense, that is, strength that comes from hearts that are united ("con-forto" – strength that comes from united hearts).

As my classmate in the seminary, I had someone who was to become a great bishop, Enrico Manfredini (for less than a year Archbishop of Bologna, where he went after being Bishop of Piacenza). I remember vividly, as I have told my friends so often, what happened one evening as we were going to the chapel. The bell had rung and we were all running down the stairs near the chapel of the theologians of the huge seminary of Venegono; we were the last two and so were rushing to catch up with the others. All at once, Manfredini took me by the arm and stopped me; I don't know how, but I looked him in the face and he said these exact words to me, which made me shudder: "To think that God became man is something out of this world!" Then I walked on and he went ahead of me. The heart of that classmate of mine was full of emotion at the greatest announcement that ever rang out in this world.

Now, by means of attentive ears and inattentive ears, receptive hearts and irritated, contrary hearts, down through centuries of history, this message is, objectively, in itself, if we repeat it and look at it, the best, most human message, most filled with promise and hope, that man can hear. Can we imagine another phrase that expresses a message better than this, more full of hope than this? No! Manfredini, my classmate, felt this in his heart; I felt it in the hand that grabbed my arm, like this, suddenly, on the staircase. "To think that God became man is something out of this world!" And while he went down the stairs faster than before, ahead of me, I shouted to him ("shouted" as loud as I dared in that period of silence), "It is something out of this world, *in* this world!" The theme this evening reminds me so readily of these things, because it asks, "How do we become Christians?" That is, how does a movement of faith come to birth in our hearts? How can a movement of faith be reborn in our hearts?

The word "heart" is, in fact, the first word we have to look at, because it brings that faith back to its origin, in that mysterious instant, in that mysterious place, in that mysterious point in which a man says, "Lord, I believe," and the Lord says, "Man, I love you." The heart is the place of the great needs: the need for truth, the need for justice, the need for love, the need – and this summarizes everything – the need for happiness. The heart, for the Bible, is this place of the great needs, which distills in the end into that shorter, more important word of all those we can say, which is the word

"I." "What use is it if you get everything you want, if you manage to have everything that comes into your head, everything, and then you lose your 'I,' your own self?" asks Jesus in the Gospel (cf. Mark 8:36; Luke 9:25).

I remember another fact from when I was in the seminary. I was reading a book by Fr Gemelli, entitled *Franciscanism*. Every chapter began with a rubric (the chapter began with a large illuminated letter, called a "rubric"). This particular chapter began with the letter Q and the Q was all illuminated. Inside the oval of the Q was the silhouette of St Francis of Assisi, with his arms open wide and his head back, and before him the faraway outline of a mountain, behind which the sun was rising, and the tail of the Q was a little bird. The first "Q" of the chapter (it began with the word "Quando") began another phrase that was written small at the feet of St Francis. This phrase made a lasting impression on me: *Quid animo satis*?[2] What can be enough to satisfy man's heart?

The symbol was clear; the most distinguished man, the man who best exemplifies the sensitivity of our race, before the finest panorama of nature and the rising sun, felt his heart wide open, and his arms were spread wide to imitate the feeling of his heart. In that moment, nothing seemed to be lacking, but actually everything was still lacking. "What can be enough to satisfy man's heart?"

[...]

St Paul once went to speak in the place in Athens where all the great philosophers and all the great politicians of the time met. In his speech on human religiosity, he said that man is in search of the meaning of his life, that is, of God, of the Other without whom he cannot understand himself; he is searching, "groping" for God (Acts 17:27) in the night, in the darkness.

[...]

Let's imagine that, all of a sudden, something extraordinary happens, what my friend Manfredini said to me: a man, a man who had been small, who had played as a child, who had sucked milk from his mother's breast, who had companions, who now and again came out with something so exceptionally intelligent that it left even adults astonished, like the doctors of the law in the Temple; then, when he had grown up, dared to say before everyone, "I am the way, the truth and the life" (John 14:6). It was an event that was therefore absolutely unforeseeable, unthinkable, not deducible from previous factors, because his father and mother were two human beings, like the others. And it is the only case, unique in history, because the prophets or religious geniuses, since they had a strong sense of the difference between man and God, had a deep perception of their limitation, of their unworthiness. At most, when they are truly great geniuses, in particular prophets sent by God into the world, they say, "This is the way to the truth." No one ever dreamed of saying, "I am the way, the truth and the life."

What if a man like this should come? He has come; a man of this kind did come, an unforeseen, unforeseeable event, not a consequence of what came before him. And for those who met him, what a wonder, what astonishment, how struck they were! They were struck by an unlimited exceptionality. It is exactly what happened to those who saw him in the first moment in which he decided to make himself known.

It is told in a passage of the Gospel that I read almost every day, the first chapter of St John's Gospel (cf. 1 John: 35–9). It describes the scene of St John the Baptist, who had foreseen the coming of the Messiah and was travelling around the desert near Jerusalem, preaching about the great event that God was about to bring about. The people were all going to listen to him, even the scribes and the Pharisees, and the heads of the people, too. Let's imagine, among all those people who were there that morning, two who were from far away, from a far-off village. They were two simple men, who made their living fishing. They were there open-mouthed, listening to John the Baptist. At a certain point, one who was in the group left and went off along the path beside the river Jordan. All of a sudden, John interrupted what he was saying and, pointing to that man who was walking away, cried out, "That is the lamb of God who takes away the sin of the world; He is the salvation of the world." They were all used to hearing the prophet explode, now and again, in phrases they didn't understand, mysterious phrases; so they weren't surprised much at this. But those two, simple men, who were all intent on listening to John the Baptist, noticed this signal, and went off to follow that young man who was going away. They followed him. They followed him for a while and didn't dare... they didn't know what to do, until he, that man, turned around and said, "What are you looking for?" "Master, where do you live?" "Come and see." They went with him and stayed with him the whole day. It was about the tenth hour. The Gospel notes the moment he appeared, the moment they saw him and went after him, the moment they came away: "It was the tenth hour." It is a note written by one of those two, John, the young man; the other, Andrew, was already married. Let's imagine those two, those two men, who spent hours there listening to that man, watching that man speaking. I don't know how much they understood of what he said, but they saw him speaking in a way that transformed them. It was something never seen, never heard, that sound of his voice, and what that voice was saying, even though they didn't really understand it, and reported some fragment of something they already knew, had already heard, like, for example, "I am the Messiah," as he said. They felt themselves above all transformed by him. Imagine how they went away that evening, how they went home. It's easy to imagine they walked home in silence. Then, when he entered his house, Andrew had such a different look on his face that his wife asked him, "What's up with you this evening?" And Andrew, without answering her, took her in his arms and embraced her in a way that almost frightened her, because he had never embraced her in such a tender, true way before. The relationship with that man had this effect, a transformation. A man was no longer the same as before; he could still go wrong like before, more than before, but he was changed.

13   You Are the Living Fountain of Hope

"MARY, THE FIRST DWELLING OF GOD IN THE WORLD"
Perché la Chiesa [Why the Church?], (Milan: Rizzoli,
2003), 307–10

*For Fr Giussani, the Christian journey, and therefore the
human journey, is destined to remain hopelessly incomprehensible without looking to the one whom God chose to make Himself present among men and women.* Verbum caro hic factum
est, *the Mystery which was beyond man's grasp was made flesh
in the womb of a woman – Mary, God's first earthly dwelling
place – through her "yes" to the message of the angel. Because
this young Hebrew girl said "yes," the Word was made flesh,
becoming a sign of hope for the world, as Dante's "Hymn to the
Virgin Mary," proclaims: "Here you are for us the midday /
torch of charity, and below among / mortals you are the living
fountain of hope."*

Christianity is the announcement of the Christ event,
of God who has come into the world as man. The mystery is no longer the "unknowable." In the Christian

sense, "mystery" is the source of being, God, in as much as He makes himself available to experience through a human reality. This concrete mode can no longer be eliminated, and remains crucial for everyone and forever. The Church is the continuity of the event of the Incarnation in history, and it is what makes it possible for man today to relate with Christ. We cannot however speak of the Church without looking at the woman from whom it is born and continues to be born, Mary, Mother of Christ.

Our Lady was chosen to be and to create the first dwelling, the first temple of God in the world, of the true, living God. She was chosen to be the first house of God, the first context, the first milieu, the first place in which everything belonged to God, to the God who was coming to live among us.

When, in Palestine, in Nazareth, I saw the small grotto, the house where Our Lady lived, and I read a rather plain plaque on which is written, *Verbum caro hic factum est*, "*Here* the Word was made flesh," I was astonished and, as it were, petrified at the unexpected evidence of God's method, who took nothing, really nothing, so as to enter history. The Word was made flesh in the entrails of a fifteen- or seventeen-year old girl, just like each one of us was flesh in his mother's womb.

Through Our Lady's motherhood God became part of human experience, of the experience of the human "I" and of its every action. It is through Mary that all the renewal of the world passes. As the election of the chosen people passed through Abraham, so the new definitive people of God, to which Christ has called us to belong, passes through a girl's womb, a woman's flesh.

So Mary is the mother of the living, and for all men happiness passes and will pass through her flesh and, even before that, through her heart, her yes, her *fiat*.

Mary's *fiat* is abandonment to the Mystery, and it marks the perfect justice of a creature before its Creator, the acknowledgment of a Presence greater than itself – this is faith. In Mary faith is expressed by her *fiat*, which is like a breath, like nothing, just as that little girl was nothing. This enormous feat, without which the whole history of the universe would be quite different, was like a breath! *Fiat*, the breath of freedom. And freedom is the capacity to adhere to being, to the Mystery that invades our life. *Fiat*, "yes."

In the impenetrable intimacy of this act of free acceptance lies the keystone in the mysterious encounter between God and Mary, and the gigantic stature of this Woman "blessed amongst women," of this victorious voyager on the human journey, *ut gigas ad currendam viam* (Ps 18:6 *Vulgate*). *Fiat*: I adhere to You, Lord. What freedom Mary had before the absolutely extraordinary thing that was happening to her, and on which the whole world's destiny depended!

What is most striking when one reads the Gospel account of the Annunciation is when the Angel finishes speaking and Our Lady says, "Yes, let it be done to me according to your word." "And the Angel left her" (Luke 1:38). Just think of the loneliness, even psychological, that girl felt in the new circumstances in which the Lord had put her, with no one else knowing what had happened, and with nothing to cling to, no common human evidence to support her. She had no apparent motivation but fidelity to her memory. She could have said, "It was an illusion, it was only my imagination."

"And the Angel left her." Faith is precisely that strength, full of attention with which the soul adheres to the sign that God has used, and clings steadfastly to this sign, despite everything. In this we grasp the summit of faith, made of the truth of reason, of faithfulness to one's own history (to what had just happened) and faithfulness to God's greatness, a hint of which had reached her with evidence.

Man's greatness is in faith, in acknowledging the great Presence within a human reality.

Since she said yes to the mode with which the Mystery was acting, her life is a light of dawn for all of us and for all men till the end of time, as Dante summarized wonderfully in his Hymn to the Virgin Mary: "Here you are for us the midday torch of charity, and below among mortals you are the living fountain of hope."

She was able to say yes, and so the Word was made flesh and became a Presence.

Our Lady introduces us into the Mystery, that is, into the meaning of our days, into the meaning of time as it runs on; her watchful care guides us on our way, her example educates us, her figure is the pattern of our resolution. A generous Mother, she generates the great Presence of Christ for us. We are consoled, forgiven, comforted, fed, enriched and gladdened by that Presence which is reborn from Our Lady's flesh. This is why we ask her every day to give us a share in her freedom, in her promptness, in her path.

The most synthetic and suggestive formula that expresses the Church's self-awareness as the ongoing presence of Christ in history is: *Veni Sancte Spiritus, veni per Mariam*. This invocation affirms God's chosen method and expresses the ardent desire for a coincidence between the relationship with Christ, who is generated in the Spirit, and reality, which is that woman's womb. *Veni Sancte Spiritus, veni per Mariam*: what happened two thousand years ago is recomposed and repeated in all the relationships that fix the pattern of men's lives and the pattern that is in history, that is, the history of God within the history of the world.

Notes

INTRODUCTION

1 L. Giussani in A. Savorana, *Vita di don Giussani* [Life of Fr Giussani] (Milan: Rizzoli, 2013), 1106.
2 "In Love with Christ. In an Encounter, the Road," Homily of Cardinal Joseph Ratzinger, Prefect of the Congregation for the Doctrine of the Faith, as cited by A. Savozana, ibid., 1188–9.
3 Ibid., 23.
4 Ibid., 8.
5 Ibid., 62.
6 Ibid., ix.
7 Ibid., 43.
8 Ibid., 1188.
9 Ibid., 47.
10 Ibid., 1188.
11 Ibid., 47.
12 Giussani as cited by Enrico Manfredini in *La conoscenza di Gesù* [Knowledge of Jesus] (Genoa-Milan: Marietti, 2004), 8, 16.
13 Savorana, *Vita di don Giussani* [Life of Father Giussani], 110.
14 L. Giussani, *The Religious Sense* (Montreal & Kingston: McGill-Queen's University Press, 1997), 9.
15 L. Giussani, *Il rischio educativo* [The Risk of Education] (Milan: Rizzoli, 2005), 20–1.

16 Savorana, *Vita di don Giussani* [Life of Father Giussani], 146.

17 Ibid., 756–7.

18 Ibid., 162.

19 Ibid., 163.

20 Ibid., 167, 221.

21 Ibid., 51.

22 Ibid., 104.

23 John Paul II, "Letter to the Reverend Monsignor Luigi Giussani, 11 February 2002," in L. Giussani, *The Work of the Movement: The Fraternity of Communion and Liberation* (Milan: Nuovo Mondo, 2005), 6.

24 Savorana, *Vita di don Giussani* [Life of Father Giussani], 1189.

25 *Evangelii Gaudium* [The Joy of the Gospel] (United States Conference of Catholic Bishops, 13 December 2013), sec. 3.

26 Savorana, *Vita di don Giussani* [Life of Father Giussani], 1028.

27 "Intervention at the Synod of Bishops on the Laity, Rome," 9 October 1987, in L. Giussani, *L'avvenimento Cristiano* [The Christian Event] (Milan: BUR, 2003), 23–5.

28 *A Generative Thought: An Introduction to the Works of Luigi Giussani*, ed. Elisa Buzzi (Montreal & Kingston: McGill-Queen's University Press, 2003), 79.

29 L. Giussani, *Un evento reale nella vita dell'uomo* [A Real Event in Human Life], (Milan: BUR, 2013), 296.

30 Offertory Prayer of the ancient liturgy for the Feast of the Sacred Heart of Jesus, *Ambrosian Missal, Easter to Advent* (Milan, 1942), 225.

CHAPTER ONE

1 Abraham Joshua Heschel, *God in Search of Man* (New York: Farrar, Straus & Giroux, 1955), 251, 253.

CHAPTER THREE

1 Graham Greene, *The End of the Affair* (London: Penguin Books, 1958).

CHAPTER FOUR

1 Henri de Lubac, *Catholicism: Christ and the Common Destiny of Man*, trans. L.C. Sheppard and E. Englund (San Francisco: Ignatius Press, 1988), 76.

CHAPTER FIVE

1 *Realtà e giovinezza: La sfida* [Youth and Reality: The Challenge] (Turin: SEI, 1995), 165.
2 See "Imitation," vol. 1, in G. Leopardi, *Canti*, trans. and annot. by Jonathan Galassi (New York: Farrar, Straus & Giroux, 2010), 311.

CHAPTER SEVEN

1 Messale Ambrosiano, vol. II (Milan: Rizzoli, 1942), 225; cf. also I Chr 29:17–18).
2 Henrik Ibsen, *Brand* (London: Penguin Classics, 1997).
3 St Thérèse of Lisieux, *Storia di un'anima* (Milan: Ancora, 1997), 291. Published in English translation as *Story of a Soul: The Autobiography* (Washington, DC: ICS Publications, 1997).

CHAPTER EIGHT

1 Ireneo di Lione, *Contro le eresie* [Against Heresy], ed. A. Cosentino (Rome: Città Nuova, 2009), IV: 20,7; English-language edition: *St. Irenaeus of Lyons against the Heresies*, trans. and anno. Dominic J. Unger, with further revisions by John J. Dillon (New York: Paulist Press), 2012.

CHAPTER NINE

1 In this regard a quotation from St Ambrose can help. In his long comment on the Creation, when he reaches the seventh day, the day God rested, he affirms, "I thank the Lord our God who created such a marvellous work in which to find his rest. He

created heaven, and I don't read that he rested; he created the earth, and I don't read that he rested; he created the sun, the moon, the stars, and I don't read that he rested even then, but I read that he created man and at this point he rested, having a being whose sins he could forgive." St Ambrose, *Exameron*, IX, 76, in *Opera omnia di Sant'Ambrogio* [The Complete Works of St Ambrose], vol. 1 (Milan-Rome: Biblioteca Ambrosiana-Città Nuova Editrice, 1979), 419.

2 Cf. O. Milosz, *Miguel Manara* (Milan: Jaca Book, 1998), 48–63.

CHAPTER TEN

1 Giussani is referring to an annual gathering of university students of Communion and Liberation that takes place at the Charterhouse of Pavia on Holy Thursday. During the morning, there are readings of chapters 14 to 17 of St John's Gospel.

2 Giussani, *At the Origin of the Christian Claim*, 80–98.

3 "This day of our Easter rejoicing, / Our innocence He will renew." From the Sunday morning hymn, "The morn dawns refulgent with glory." In *Book of Hours* (Milan: Coop. Edit. Nuovo Mondo, 2009), 992.

CHAPTER TWELVE

1 See Didaché, *Dottrina dei dodici apostoli* [The Teaching of the Twelve Apostles], with Greek parallel text (Cinisello balsamo: San Paolo Edizioni, 2003), IV: 2; see also English-language edition: *Didachè: The Unknown Teaching of the Twelve Apostles*, ed. Brent S. Walters, (San José, CA: Ante-Nicene Archive, 1991).

2 Cf. A. Gemelli, *Il Francescanesimo* (Milan: Edizioni O.R., 1932), ch. 13; published in English as *The Franciscan Message to the World*, (London: Burns, Oates & Co., 1934), ch. 13.

Permissions

Material published for the first time in English has been translated by Kristin Hurd. Works previously published in English translation are from the following works.

Alla ricerca del volto umano
Rizzoli: Milano 1995
pp. 141–5; 147, 149–52; 153
Translated by Kristin Hurd

At the Origin of the Christian Claim
McGill-Queen's University Press 1999
pp. 29–3, 34
Translated by Viviane Hewitt

Come si diventa cristiani
Marietti *1820*: Genua-Milan 2007
pp. 9–23
Translated by Patrick Stevenson

L. Giussani, S. Alberto, and J. Prades
Generating Traces in the History of the World
McGill-Queen's University Press 1998
pp. ix–xii, 59–63
Translated by Patrick Stevenson

"The Glory of God Is Man Who Lives"
Msgr Luigi Giussani's closing talk at the retreat of the Fraternity
of Communion and Liberation,
Rimini, 5 May 2002
Translated by Susan Scott

Il rischio educativo
Rizzoli: Milano 2005
pp. 15–21
Translated by Kristin Hurd

Is It Possible to Live This Way?, vol. 3 *Charity*
McGill-Queen's University Press 2009
pp. 7–18
Edited by John Zucchi

The Journey to Truth Is an Experience
McGill-Queen's University Press 2006
pp. 53–7
Translated and annotated by John Zucchi with the assistance of
Patrick Stevenson

Perché la Chiesa
Rizzoli: Milano 2003
pp. 307–10
Translated by Patrick Stevenson

The Religious Sense
McGill-Queen's University Press 1997
pp. 100–1; 105–6; 108–9
Translated by John Zucchi

Uomini senza patria: 1982–1983
Rizzoli Bur: Milan 2008
pp. 8–12
Translated by Patrick Stevenson

Why the Church?
McGill-Queen's University Press 2001
pp. 5–6, 7–9; 72–3, 123–68, 154–5
Translated by Viviane Hewitt